NUTRITION AND HEALTH

FOOD SAFETY

SAVING LIVES

BY JULIANA BURKHART

Portions of this book originally appeared in
Food Regulation and Safety by Kevin Hillstrom.

D1319385

LUCENT
P R E S S

Published in 2020 by
Lucent Press, an Imprint of Greenhaven Publishing, LLC
353 3rd Avenue
Suite 255
New York, NY 10010

Designer: Deanna Paternostro
Editor: Jennifer Lombardo

Library of Congress Cataloging-in-Publication Data

Names: Burkhart, Juliana, author.
Title: Food safety : saving lives / Juliana Burkhart.
Description: New York : Lucent Press, [2020] | Series: Nutrition and health |
  Includes bibliographical references and index.
Identifiers: LCCN 2019009839 (print) | LCCN 2019014071 (ebook) | ISBN
  9781534568822 (eBook) | ISBN 9781534568716 (library bound) | ISBN
  9781534568860 (pbk.)
Subjects: LCSH: Food–Safety measures–Juvenile literature. | Foodborne
  diseases–Prevention–Juvenile literature. | Food industry and
  trade–United States–Juvenile literature.
Classification: LCC RA601 (ebook) | LCC RA601 .B87 2020 (print) | DDC
  615.9/540289–dc23
LC record available at https://lccn.loc.gov/2019009839

Printed in China

Some of the images in this book illustrate individuals who are models. The depictions do not imply actual situations or events.

CPSIA compliance information: Batch #BW20KL: For further information contact Greenhaven Publishing LLC, New York, New York at 1-844-317-7404.

Please visit our website, www.greenhavenpublishing.com. For a free color catalog of all our high-quality books, call toll free 1-844-317-7404 or fax 1-844-317-7405.

CONTENTS

FOREWORD

People often want to do whatever they can to live healthy lives, but this is frequently easier said than done. For example, experts suggest minimizing stress as it takes a long-term toll on the body and mind. However, in an era where young adults must balance school attendance, extracurricular and social activities, and several hours of homework each night, stress is virtually unavoidable. Socioeconomic factors also come into play, which can prevent someone from making good health choices even when they are aware of what the consequences will be.

Other times, however, the problem is misinformation. The media frequently reports watered-down versions of scientific findings, distorting the message and causing confusion. Sometimes multiple conflicting results are reported, leaving people to wonder whether a simple action such as eating dark chocolate is helpful, harmful, or has no effect on their health at all. In such an environment, many people ignore all health news and decide for themselves what the best course of action is. This has led to dangerous trends such as the recent anti-vaccination movement.

The titles in the Nutrition and Health series aim to give young adults the information they need to take charge of their health. Factual, unbiased text presents all sides of current health issues with the understanding that everyone is different and knows their own body and health needs best. Readers also gain insight into important nutrition topics, such as whether a vegetarian diet is right for them, which foods may improve or exacerbate any existing health issues, and precautions they can take to prevent the spread of foodborne illnesses.

Annotated quotes from medical experts provide accurate and accessible explanations of challenging concepts, as well as different points of view on controversial issues. Additional books and websites are listed, giving readers a starting point from which to delve deeper into specific topics that are of interest to them. Full-color photographs, fact boxes, and enlightening charts are presented alongside the informative text to give young adults a clearer picture of today's most pressing health concerns.

With so much complicated and conflicting information about nutrition and health available on social media and in the news, it can be hard for all people—but especially for young adults—to make smart choices about their health. However, this series presents an accessible approach to health education that makes the work of staying healthy seem much less intimidating.

GROWING CONCERN OVER FOOD SAFETY

In the United States, people have a wide variety of foods to choose from. Americans generally recognize that some of these foods are more nutritious and healthier than others, and many make their dietary selections based on those factors. Other Americans place a greater emphasis on personal taste, cost, and convenience when they decide where to dine or what to put in their grocery carts. The one consideration that rarely enters into their calculations is food safety. Most Americans take it for granted that all the foods and beverages they purchase are safe to consume.

For the most part, this faith in the safety of the nation's food supply is well-founded. Over the past century or so, government agencies at the local, state, and federal levels have put important food safety regulations and guidelines in place to minimize people's risk of encountering dangerous foodborne bacteria and other health threats. These rules have been continually revised and updated over the years to keep up with amazing technological changes in the food industry.

In recent years, though, food safety has emerged as an issue of growing public concern. Deadly outbreaks of illnesses stemming from contaminated food sources in the United States are reported by news outlets, and the stories are then widely shared online. In addition, environmental and consumer advocacy groups believe that farms, ranches, and other food sources that use a lot of pesticides, herbicides, and antibiotics are endangering public health and threatening fragile ecosystems. A heated international debate has also broken out over whether genetically modified (GM) crops and animals are safe for the environment and for human consumption.

These controversies have led critics to claim that America's food regulation system is not working as well as it should be. They believe that food safety problems need to be addressed through new safety regulations and changes in industry practices. They also propose new educational campaigns to inform consumers about the potential health benefits and drawbacks of their food choices.

The food industry, however, opposes many of these suggested reforms, believing them to be unnecessary. Food producers emphasize that tens of millions of Americans eat breakfast, lunch, dinner, and snacks every day without getting sick. Some farmers, feedlot owners, ranchers, food processors, grocery companies, and restaurant owners also argue that stricter regulatory oversight will just increase their operating expenses—which will in turn force them to raise the prices that consumers pay. This debate is likely to go on for the foreseeable future, but by doing their own research, educating themselves, and making small changes to their lifestyles, most consumers can give themselves peace of mind about their food.

FOOD SAFETY THROUGHOUT U.S. HISTORY

Imagine life as a colonial settler in early America. A child is woken by the smell of baking bread and gets up to help their mother with the morning task of collecting eggs from the family's hens. Later, the child is sent to get milk from the neighbors, who own a cow, in exchange for some beans and onions grown in their family's small garden. The milk will be used to make butter and cheese at home.

By early afternoon, the child's father has returned from the day's hunt with a wild turkey and two rabbits. The turkey is roasted for that evening's supper, while the rabbits are skinned and preserved for another meal. On special occasions, if a family could afford it, they might visit the town's butcher to purchase beef.

Fast-forward to life in 21st-century America, where people can visit a single store to shop for all of these foods and thousands more from all over the world. Unlike today, families in colonial America sustained themselves on a limited diet of foods from local sources found in nature or grown or raised by others in their community. They knew where their food was coming from, so there was no need for the government to regulate crops and livestock. However, as American towns and cities grew larger, the merchants, farmers, butchers, and fishers who controlled the food supply became less familiar to customers. A need to produce larger quantities of food at a faster pace led some people to cut corners in an effort to make more food available faster at less cost to the seller. The process of adding inferior, impure, or unnecessary ingredients came to be known as "adulteration." By the late 18th century, state and local authorities had passed several laws forbidding the practice.

Regulation of the U.S. food supply took another leap forward in the

Most people have no idea where the food in their local supermarket comes from. This is a relatively recent development in human history.

late 19th century. Scientists, doctors, and public health officials around the world made a number of important discoveries about the role that bacteria, viruses, and other microscopic germs play in causing illnesses. Armed with this knowledge, American cities and states began passing laws designed to reduce their citizens' vulnerability to disease-causing germs—also known as pathogens—lurking in their food and water supplies. They passed laws to protect drinking water from sewage contamination and launched programs to teach people about the importance of hand washing and other hygienic practices.

A Closer Look

In 1947, Michigan became the first state to require that all milk for sale within its borders be pasteurized.

Another important food safety development was the pasteurization of milk. Pasteurization was a revolutionary process invented by French scientist Louis Pasteur. He found that heating fresh milk killed the

A Serious but Uncommon Problem

Accusations of adulteration have been common ever since people began buying food from others. People accused food sellers of adding things such as candle wax to butter, sawdust to tea, and sand to sugar in an effort to stretch their supply and sell less food for more profit. In 1757, a book called *Poison Detected: Or Frightful Truths* was published by an anonymous author who accused bakers of adding crushed bones and the ashes of cremated bodies to bread. Another book published around the same time stated that bakers added other things, including chalk and white lead, to everything they made.

These accusations scared many people, but it is likely that most of them were not true. In 1934, Frederick A. Filby made bread using the materials people had claimed were used as fillers in bread and determined that the accusations could not be true. As author Bill Bryson reported of Filby's experiment, "In every case but one the bread was either as hard as concrete or failed to set at all, and nearly all the loaves smelled or tasted disgusting. Several needed more baking time than conventional loaves and so were actually more expensive to produce."[1] Food adulteration did happen, but nowhere near as commonly as it was reported.

1. Bill Bryson, *At Home: A Short History of Private Life*. New York, NY: Doubleday, 2010, pp. 67–68.

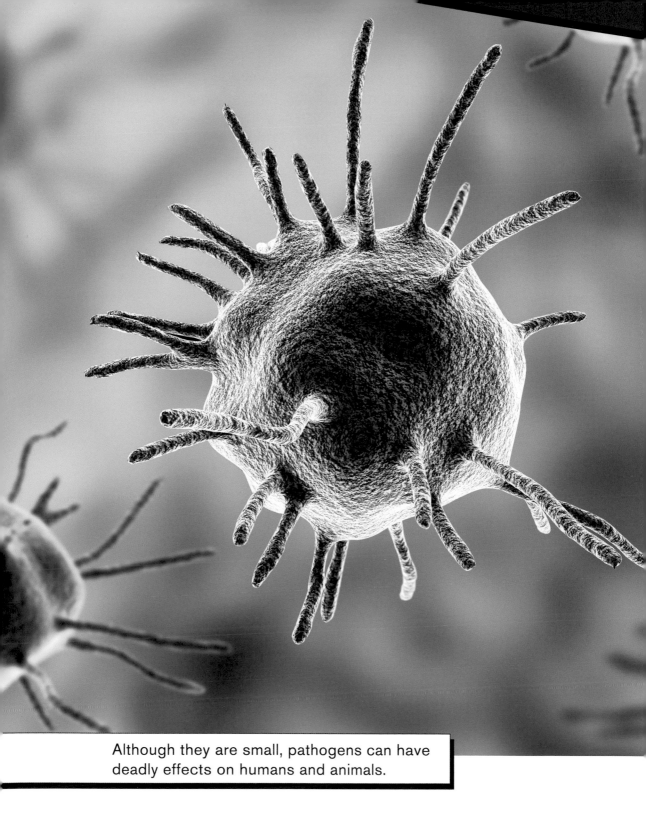

Although they are small, pathogens can have deadly effects on humans and animals.

pathogens in it that caused typhoid fever, scarlet fever, diphtheria, tuberculosis, and other diseases. Although people were slow to recognize pasteurization's health benefits, pasteurization programs were in widespread use across the United States by the 1920s. Pasteurization greatly reduced deaths and illnesses from contaminated milk, and it remains standard practice today.

The Meatpacking Industry Faces Public Outcry

Aside from the introduction of pasteurization and the rise of state food adulteration laws, there still were not many regulations concerning the preparation and sale of food at the beginning of the 20th century. In 1906, however, author Upton Sinclair published a book that dramatically changed American attitudes about the need for additional food regulation. *The Jungle* was a novel set in Chicago, Illinois, which was the center of the nation's meatpacking industry at the turn of the century. The meatpacking workers in Sinclair's book were fictional, but the conditions he described in the city's stockyards and slaughterhouses—factories where cows, hogs, and other animals are killed and converted into beef and pork products—were all too real. *The Jungle* depicted a world of appalling filth and disease—for example, rats were common in the slaughterhouses and would run over the meat before it was sold. This book made American families aware that they were being fed a steady diet of spoiled and contaminated meat.

Sinclair's book sparked a tremendous public uproar from horrified readers, and a shaken U.S. Congress acted promptly to address the

Thanks to *The Jungle*, the government began inspecting meat products for quality.

outrage. By the end of 1906, two major federal food safety bills had been signed into law by President Theodore Roosevelt. The first of these laws was the Pure Food and Drug Act. This legislation banned the transport or sale of mislabeled or adulterated food, drinks, and drugs across state lines. It also gave the U.S. Department of Agriculture's Bureau of Chemistry (known today as the Food and Drug Administration, or FDA) the authority to inspect meat products and slaughterhouse operations.

A Closer Look

According to research by the Organization for Economic Cooperation and Development (OECD), the average American eats about 200 pounds (91 kg) of meat each year.

The other major law to come out of the public outrage over *The Jungle* was the Meat Inspection Act of 1906. This legislation replaced a much weaker law that had been passed in 1890. The new law ordered the U.S. Department of Agriculture (USDA) to conduct regular inspections of slaughterhouses and meatpacking plants to make sure they followed sanitary standards and used only healthy livestock. These visual and manual inspections were not sophisticated enough to detect the presence of disease-causing bacteria in animals or meat products. They did succeed, however, in weeding out obviously sick animals and spoiled meat that meatpackers had once offered for sale to unsuspecting customers. As the quality of beef, pork, and lamb improved, rates of disease from meatborne infections steadily declined across the United States.

Mass Poisoning Sparks Tighter Regulations

Federal regulation of food did not change much from the 1910s through the mid-1930s. A few modest food-related laws and rules emerged during these years, but they were primarily concerned with labeling or governing specific parts of the rapidly expanding food industry. The Seafood Inspection Act of 1934, for example, put new FDA procedures in place for ensuring the freshness of shrimp and other seafood.

Thirty-one years after the publication of *The Jungle*, however, the American food industry was once again rocked by an event that intensified public concerns about the safety of the nation's food supply. That fall, Americans opened their newspapers and read about an unfolding tragedy that eventually claimed the lives of more than 100 people in 15 states. These fatalities were traced to "Elixir Sulfanilamide," a medicine produced and distributed by a drug manufacturer based in Tennessee.

Elixir Sulfanilamide was a liquid form of sulfanilamide, a safe and well-established drug that was commonly used to treat streptococcal, or strep, infections and other bacterial infections. Before 1937, the drug had only been available in tablet or powder form, but a Tennessee drugmaker decided that a liquid version might be even more popular. The company's chief chemist discovered that by adding a chemical known as diethylene glycol, he could dissolve sulfanilamide into liquid form. The company laboratory then added some raspberry flavoring to make the medicine more appetizing and sent more than 600 shipments of the liquid medicine to pharmacies and doctors across the country. Unfortunately, the safety of the new drug compound was never tested. When doctors began prescribing it to patients, deaths began to mount. Investigators later determined that the diethylene glycol additive was a toxic substance similar to antifreeze.

The mass poisoning prompted outpourings of fury and grief from the American public—and from doctors as well. One physician wrote that six of his patients, including his best friend, were killed after "they took medicine that I prescribed for them innocently … [not knowing that it] had become a deadly poison in its newest and most modern form … That realization has given me such days and nights of mental and spiritual agony as I did not believe a human being could undergo and survive."[1]

In the wake of this awful tragedy, Congress responded with the Food, Drug, and Cosmetic Act (FDCA) of 1938, which placed strong new regulations on the operations of drug companies. The pharmaceutical industry, though, was not the only industry to be affected by this law. Numerous provisions of the FDCA were aimed at the food industry, which had outgrown many of the safety regulations that had been crafted at the beginning of the century. The FDCA authorized the federal government to strengthen its inspections of food manufacturing and processing plants. It also gave the FDA new powers to monitor the care and treatment of livestock, set safety standards for infant formula, and make stricter food labeling requirements. Finally, the law declared that food products could be classified as "adulterated"—and thus illegal—if they contained potentially dangerous chemicals.

Agriculture and the Great Depression

At the same time that the U.S. government was expanding its oversight of the food industry, American agriculture was growing at an amazing rate. Boosted by new farming machines, improvements in overseas shipping, and innovations in refrigeration and other food preservation technologies, American farmers and ranchers were able to deliver their products to towns and cities all across the United States—and even around the world. By the early 1900s, in fact, U.S. exports of meat and grains had become so great that Americans were proudly describing their nation as the breadbasket of the world.

This decades-long run of agricultural expansion and prosperity came to a shattering stop with the arrival of the Great Depression in 1929. The Great Depression was a terrible economic crisis that produced record levels of business closures, bank failures, and unemployment in America and around the world. In the Midwest, it was made even worse by drought and dust storms in the mid-1930s. Several farm states in the Great Plains region lost millions of acres of farmland, earning the area the nickname of the Dust Bowl. When journalist Ernie Pyle toured the Dust Bowl, he reported that in many regions "there was not a tree or a blade of grass, or a dog or a cow or a human being—nothing whatsoever, nothing at all but gray raw earth and a few farmhouses and barns, sticking up from the dark gray sea like white cattle skeletons on the desert ... [It was] the saddest land I have ever seen."[2]

President Franklin D. Roosevelt responded to the Great Depression with a wave of new laws and programs known collectively as the New Deal. Several New Deal policies were crafted, as author Michael Pollan noted, "to rescue farmers from the disastrous effects of growing too much food—far more than Americans

Dust storms threatened the lives and businesses of people who lived in the American Midwest in the 1930s, so thousands of people had to move to other parts of the country just to survive. Shown here is a Dust Bowl refugee family in the truck they made their temporary home.

could afford to buy."[3] This oversupply of food was keeping crop, dairy, and livestock prices so low that farmers could not survive. The U.S. government addressed this problem by paying farmers to slaughter huge numbers of livestock and buying up excess corn and other crops for storage. In addition, the government began paying some farmers not to grow crops. These payments allowed farmers to receive an income while at the same time keeping supplies of wheat, corn, and other crops from rising to a point where they would cause a crash in crop prices.

The Big Business of Farming

America's economy pulled out of the Depression after World War II. Since farmers were now better protected from the threat of low crop prices, farms could grow bigger without fear of financial ruin. Small farmers, though, had difficulty keeping up in this environment, which rewarded big operations that could afford new technologies such as pesticides, fertilizers, mechanical milking machines, and tractors.

The push toward "mega farms" in the United States further intensified in the 1970s,

Corn is one of America's biggest cash crops. In addition to being a common food item, it can be used to make many nonedible products. For example, corn oil is used in many soaps, and ethanol, a fuel source made from distilled corn, is often blended with gasoline to make cars more eco-friendly.

when the federal government replaced New Deal farm policies with a system that encouraged farmers to plant as much as they possibly could and to use herbicides, pesticides, fertilizers, and anything else that would boost their yields of corn, wheat, soybeans, apples, and other foods. Producers of beef, pork, and other meat products got the same message.

Supporters of these new policies believed that increasing America's food supply would make prices go down in butcher shops and grocery stores around the country, which would make food more affordable for the average consumer. They were right—food prices did drop. However, the new system made it harder for family farms to survive unless they concentrated on growing one or two of the most valuable commodity crops—generally corn, wheat, or soybeans. Big farming corporations, on the other hand, thrived in this environment. Armed with lots of money, they invested heavily in new technologies that allowed them to grow and produce food at an unprecedented rate.

Technology to Increase Production

As agricultural technology grew, scientists developed methods to cause genetic changes to crop seeds that made the plants resistant to the powerful herbicides that had entered the market. The goal was to help farmers kill weeds without accidentally killing their own plants. They even grew plants with genes that produced their own insecticides, which increased the growing capacity of crops. Commercial use of these genetically modified (GM) seeds (also known as transgenic or bioengineered seeds) soared after 1992, when the FDA formally approved their use. Two years later, the first commercial GM food product—the Flavr Savr tomato—was shipped to American grocery stores. The push toward GM seeds intensified after that, especially since easily modifiable crops such as corn and soybeans are used as ingredients in so many different processed foods. As of 2019, as much as 80 percent of processed food products that are sold in the United States contain GM ingredients that the FDA has said are safe for people to eat. The most commonly engineered crops, according to *Huffpost*, are corn, soy, squash, zucchini, alfalfa, canola, and sugar beets.

Producers of beef, pork, poultry, and dairy products also became steadily more dependent on scientific advances in agriculture. Most notably, they dramatically expanded their use of growth hormones and other government-approved chemicals that increased the size of their chickens, cows, and hogs. Use of antibiotics—bacteria-fighting medications—also surged in the meat industry during the 1970s and 1980s. The increased reliance on antibiotics stemmed from the fact that cows, chickens, and other animals were increasingly kept in crowded warehouses, where they could be raised and slaughtered cheaply. Since large numbers of animals confined in such close quarters are at greater risk of spreading disease, heavy application of antibiotics became a fast and inexpensive way for feedlot operators to reduce the risk of a disease outbreak.

Within the food industry, these massive facilities are called concentrated animal feeding operations (CAFOs). Among critics, however, CAFOs are known as "factory farms," and during the 1980s and 1990s, environmental protection groups and consumer advocacy organizations condemned them for multiple reasons. Opponents of factory farms claimed that the huge amounts of animal waste generated in CAFOs posed a pollution threat to local rivers, lakes, and underground water supplies. They also said that these operations treated animals inhumanely. Additionally, critics expressed alarm about the heavy volume of antibiotics that were being introduced into America's chickens, cows, and pigs in these operations. They warned that excessive reliance on antibiotics might eventually create frightening new antibiotic-resistant strains of pathogens that could sicken or even kill humans if they entered the food supply. People have also expressed concern about how eating meat from animals treated with antibiotics can affect humans' health. However, experts say that the laws in place in the United States and other countries that food is imported from ensure that animal products are not contaminated with antibiotics. According to the website Healthline, "Drug withdrawal periods are enforced before treated animals, eggs or milk are used as food. This allows time for the drugs to completely leave the animal's system. The US Department of Agriculture (USDA) has a strict process of testing all meat, poultry, eggs and milk for unwanted compounds, including antibiotic residues."[4]

Ingredient Labeling

Local and state lawmaking bodies frantically tried to keep pace with the rapid industrialization of the food industry. They crafted new policies and laws to better ensure that farmers, livestock operations, and big food-processing companies were marketing their products honestly, raising their crops and animals responsibly, and producing food that was safe to eat. Several states, for example, passed laws that either prohibited the establishment of new factory farms or imposed new environmental and public health restrictions on their operations.

New food regulations also were introduced at the national level to better protect consumers. The 1990 Nutrition Labeling and Education Act (NLEA) required all packaged foods to contain standardized information on their nutritional content. It was followed six years later by the Food Quality Protection Act (FQPA). This law gave the U.S. Environmental Protection Agency (EPA) the power to impose new safety standards for pesticide use. "If a pesticide poses a danger to our children, then it won't be in our food," declared President Bill Clinton when he signed the act into law. "I like to think of it as the 'peace of mind act,' because it will give parents the peace of mind that comes from knowing that fruits, vegetables and grains they put down in front of their children are safe."[5]

In 2004, Congress passed the Food Allergen Labeling and Consumer Protection Act (FALCPA). This law required manufacturers to clearly label packaged foods that contained any ingredients made from the eight foods that account for most food allergies: milk, eggs, fish, shellfish, tree nuts, peanuts, wheat, and soybeans.

Despite all these new laws, however, the safety of America's food supply remained in question. Although federal health regulations had been shored up to better protect consumers from fraudulent advertising, toxic additives, and pesticides, there was still the issue of foodborne bacteria such as *Salmonella*, *Listeria*, *Campylobacter*, and *Escherichia coli*, better known as *E. coli*.

Industrialization and Foodborne Illness

Although these pathogens have always been around, they were generally not considered a major concern until the 1970s. Food safety experts and scientists believe that modern food production techniques have contributed to making these germs more widespread. "More and more animals are raised on a single farm, so hundreds of thousands of pigs, or hundreds of thousands of chickens, may be raised under one roof. This gives the opportunity for pathogens to spread from one animal to another," explained Dr. Robert Tauxe, director of the foodborne diseases division at the Centers for Disease Control and Prevention (CDC). He continued,

> [W]hen they are transported to slaughter, animals from many different farms may go in the same truck or the same transport freight to the slaughterhouse. Again, there's the opportunity for the exchange of these bacteria. As the line speeds and the general efficiency of the slaughter plants increase, there may also be a greater opportunity for contamination to spread from one carcass to another. I suspect that the industrialization of our meat supply opened up a conduit for ... infections to pass through to the consumer.[6]

Experts also emphasize that once food has been tainted with harmful pathogens—generally by direct contact with infected animals' waste or stomach contents during slaughtering or processing—outbreaks are very difficult to contain. Although cuts of meat such as steaks come from just one animal, ground meat such as sausage or hamburger patties routinely contains meat trimmings from dozens or even hundreds of different cows. If even one of those cows carried *E. coli* or *Salmonella*, then thousands of pounds of hamburger are at risk of contamination. "The meatpacking system that arose to supply the nation's fast food chains—an industry molded to serve their needs, to provide massive amounts of uniform ground beef so that all of McDonald's hamburgers would taste the same—has proved to be an extremely efficient system for spreading disease,"[7] wrote investigative journalist Eric Schlosser.

Finally, the potential for outbreaks of foodborne illness has risen due to the sophistication of America's transportation system. "High-speed distribution means contaminated food can be in consumers' homes, and stomachs, long before the contamination is detected," explained journalist Paul Roberts. "The very innovations that let us feed so many so well can also nourish an epidemic—and ensure that its impacts will be devastating."[8]

Twentieth-Century Epidemics Cause Panic

In 1985, foodborne illnesses became a major news story when *Salmonella*-tainted milk killed 2 and sickened another 16,284 people.

Farm animals that are kept in close quarters are highly likely to spread disease.

Most of them lived in the Chicago area near the infected dairy. That same year, an outbreak of *Listeria* in soft cheese claimed 48 lives in southern California.

These outbreaks were greatly alarming to farmers, scientists, and public health officials, in part because pathogen-infected livestock did not show any outward symptoms. Contaminated cattle looked and behaved just the same as ones that were not carrying the pathogens. "We had always believed that if you kept the livestock from getting sick, the food was safe," said Lester Crawford, who worked in the USDA's meat inspection department and later served as chief of the FDA. "The phrase we used was 'healthy livestock, healthy people.' But here was a case where livestock were thriving and people were getting not just sick, but *violently* sick."[9]

Mad Cow Disease Outbreak

In 1986, British public health authorities identified a frightening new and fatal brain disease that was spreading across that nation's cattle population. Called "mad cow disease" because infected animals appeared aggressive and disoriented, the disease was officially named bovine spongiform encephalopathy (BSE). The discovery of BSE was enormously damaging to the British beef industry, which had to destroy huge numbers of cattle in an effort to stop the outbreak.

In 1996, investigators discovered that humans who ate BSE-infected meat could actually contract a deadly form of the disease. The knowledge that mad cow disease was capable of transmitting from cattle to humans prompted the U.S. government to impose a wide range of new anti-BSE regulations, including bans on certain cattle feeds linked to the disease and bans on the processing of "downer" cows (those too sick to stand or walk) for food.

Fortunately, BSE is rare: U.S. public health authorities have identified only six cases of mad cow disease in America. The most recent of these came in 2018, when officials determined that a cow in Florida was suffering from the disease.

Reports of food poisoning from pathogens increased steadily through the late 1980s and early 1990s, but it was not until late 1992 that another major outbreak made the national news. In December of that year, doctors in the Seattle, Washington, area observed a sudden surge in emergency room visits from children suffering from bloody diarrhea and rare kidney problems. Investigators eventually traced the problem to undercooked hamburgers from the Jack in the Box fast food chain. These hamburgers, which were contaminated with E. coli bacteria, killed four children and sickened more than 700 people up and down the West Coast before the outbreak was contained in February 1993.

The stories of the children who died from the Jack in the Box outbreak caused an outpouring of grief and outrage from the public. Five-year-old Lauren Rudolph's parents had taken her to a San Diego–area Jack in the Box just before Christmas as a reward for getting good grades on her report card. Three days after Christmas, the first-grader was dead, a victim of E. coli bacteria. Author Nicols Fox noted that "no one at the hospital had thought to run the standard tests for [E. coli] while Lauren was alive. If they had ... the future for more than seven hundred other people might have been different."[10]

Tragedy Prompts Demand for Legislation

After the Jack in the Box outbreak, American consumers demanded action from their government. The USDA responded to the Jack in the Box crisis by imposing significant new safety regulations. The organization classified E. coli as an adulterant—the first time a bacteria had ever been given this designation. This new classification meant that the meat industry would have to take the same anti-contamination measures against the pathogen that it already did against toxins that could be deliberately added to food. It also approved a new meat safety monitoring system called Hazard Analysis and Critical Control Point (HACCP).

Under HACCP regulations, meat-processing companies were forced to improve their food safety procedures and invest in new food safety technologies. Testing of food quality at various points in processing operations became routine. If food-production companies failed to meet federal safety standards for pathogens, the USDA had the power to pull its inspectors out of their facilities. If no inspectors were present, then the company could not obtain a "USDA Inspected" stamp for its products. Since these stamps were required by grocery stores, food companies had to police themselves if they wanted to keep their inspectors working.

The introduction of HACCP undoubtedly improved meat quality and safety. As time passed, though, some consumer advocates and USDA food safety regulators complained that the system, which made food companies responsible for carrying out HACCP programs, still did not provide enough safeguards. They argued that food makers still sometimes ignored safety regulations if the regulations reduced financial profitability. As one former USDA meat inspector put it, when companies are allowed to take on food safety responsibilities without sufficient government oversight, "it's like the wolf guarding the henhouse."[11]

More Disease Outbreaks in the United States

The new safety regulations failed to protect the United States from another wave of disease outbreaks caused by foodborne pathogens. In 1994, *Salmonella*-tainted ice cream sickened thousands of people in more than 30 states. Two years later, an *E. coli* outbreak that sickened 66 people and killed a 16-month-old girl was traced to unpasteurized apple juice. In 1998, *Listeria*-tainted deli meats and hot dogs that had been produced at a Pennsylvania food-processing plant were linked to 21 deaths and more than 100 illnesses in almost two dozen states.

By the start of the new millennium, growing numbers of American consumers were expressing mounting concern—and sometimes outright alarm—about whether the food they were feeding their families was safe. These worries further intensified as reports of additional outbreaks kept coming. In 2000, 65 people were sickened and a three-year-old girl died when 2 Milwaukee-area restaurants in Wisconsin served undercooked beef infected with *E. coli*. One year later, more than 100 million pounds of meat were recalled on the suspicion that the meat was infected. In 2003, green onions that had been imported from Mexico and used at a Chi-Chi's Mexican Restaurant in Pennsylvania sickened more than 600 customers and killed 4 people. Investigators later found that the onions were infected with the hepatitis A virus. In the summer of 2006, an outbreak of *E. coli* was caused by spinach, which investigators believed had been contaminated from irrigation water that contained cattle feces. By the time the outbreak was contained, 3 people were dead and nearly 200 more had been sickened. In 2008, a salmonellosis—*Salmonella* infection—outbreak from processed peanut butter killed 9 people and sickened at least 714 others. Two years later, more than 1,500 illnesses from *Salmonella* were traced to two egg farms in Iowa, prompting a recall of 500 million eggs across more than a dozen states. In 2011, *Listeria*-contaminated cantaloupes from Colorado killed 33 people and sickened a total of 147 people in 28 states. In 2018, 210 people across 36 states became ill from *E. coli* transmitted in romaine lettuce, and 5 deaths were reported from that incident.

Modernizing Food Safety for the 21st Century

For many years, American agribusiness—a term that encompasses all of the various sectors of the food industry—was able to use its political influence to stop many suggested reforms that it feared would increase operating costs and decrease profits. Even after the 1992–1993 Jack in the Box outbreak convinced U.S. authorities to take new steps to combat *E. coli*, the meat industry managed to fight off calls for regulations that would target other foodborne bacteria, such as *Salmonella* and *Listeria*.

Food safety advocates did not give up, though. They continued to press for additional regulations, and in 2010, Congress passed the biggest overhaul of America's food-safety laws since the 1930s. The bill, officially known as the FDA Food Safety Modernization Act (FSMA), was signed into law by President Barack Obama on January 4, 2011. The law affects all whole and processed foods except meat, poultry, and some egg products, all of which are regulated by the USDA rather than the FDA. The FSMA requires the food industry to make new investments in bacteria-fighting technology and gives the FDA full authority to recall tainted food, increase inspections of farms and food-processing facilities, and create a food-tracking system that will allow authorities to quickly identify the source of outbreaks from foodborne pathogens. To be in compliance with the law, food companies must keep documentation of their food-safety plans and give the FDA access to these records. The FSMA also gave the FDA authority to prohibit a facility from distributing food if it determines that the food poses a reasonable risk to public health. Furthermore, the FSMA gave the FDA greater authority over imported products, including requiring importers to verify that foreign food suppliers have taken adequate measures to ensure their products are safe.

Food safety advocates were happy with the law, believing that America had taken a major step forward in improving the quality and safety of its food supply. "This is a big victory for consumers that finally brings food-safety laws into the 21st century," proclaimed Jean Halloran of Consumers Union. "This win is a powerful testament to the people across the country who came to Washington to tell their lawmakers how contaminated food had killed their loved ones or left them horribly sick. This win is for them and all Americans."[12]

Chapter Two

FOOD SAFETY AGENCIES IN THE UNITED STATES

The United States has put in place a network of agencies and institutions charged with protecting its citizens' food supply. Governmental food safety organizations operate on local, state, and federal levels. However, citizens themselves also have a voice in how the nation's food safety issues are handled. In addition, scientists, public health advocates, small farmers, and big agribusinesses contribute to the discussion on policies regarding the regulation of foods and beverages. Sometimes these agencies and organizations compete with differing perspectives; other times, they work together to achieve common goals.

Local Authorities

Local agencies carry out a wide range of duties to monitor food safety in their communities. Their exact responsibilities vary from town to town, county to county, and region to region, but in general, they act as the first line of defense against foodborne disease outbreaks, contamination of food and water supplies from industrial toxins, and other threats. Local agencies and inspectors, in fact, carry out the great majority of food safety inspections that take place in the United States every year. "[Local] inspectors routinely look for sanitation problems, temperature problems with refrigerated or stored foods, and employee sanitation concerns, such as personal hygiene among food handlers," wrote James T. O'Reilly in his book *A Consumer's Guide to Food Regulation & Safety*. "Closing filthy restaurant kitchens or ordering destruction of a truckload of defrosted meat in a broken trailer does not get headline news coverage, but this phase of real consumer protection is vitally important."[13]

Funding and political support varies wildly for the estimated 3,000 local public health agencies that are involved in food safety issues affecting their communities. Some local agencies benefit from steady administrative leadership, generous and reliable funding, and strong community support. Other agencies take a less active role, either because they do not have enough funding or because local politicians and businesses oppose them. In general, however, local health departments and food inspection agencies have the following food safety responsibilities:

- collecting and responding to local food safety consumer complaints
- performing laboratory tests on potentially contaminated food and food sources
- responding to local outbreaks of foodborne illness
- licensing and inspecting food safety standards at local grocery stores, restaurants, and other establishments that sell food and drinks
- providing technical training and education on food safety issues

State Authorities

State-level public health, environmental, and consumer protection agencies also provide a variety of food safety functions. They often undertake these responsibilities in cooperation with federal food safety agencies. For example, more than 80 percent of the inspections of meat and poultry processing operations across the United States are actually carried out by state agencies. These inspections, however, are conducted on behalf of the USDA, which sets the food safety standards that the businesses must meet. States are generally responsible for carrying out the following food safety functions:

- issuing recalls of food and drink products that are found to pose a threat to public health
- monitoring for outbreaks of foodborne illness at all stages of food production, from the farm to the dinner table
- performing laboratory tests to identify food-related pathogens
- setting standards for cleanliness and safe treatment of food products in grocery stores and restaurants; some state agencies also carry out inspections of these facilities

Any food can potentially be contaminated, which is why all food must be inspected.

- inspecting farming operations to enforce regulations on animal health and the use of pesticides and herbicides
- providing technical training and education on food safety issues

Federal Agencies

At the national level, responsibility for food safety is divided among four federal agencies. Many people know that the FDA, which is part of the U.S. Department of Health and Human Services (HHS), oversees the safety and security of drugs, medical devices, and cosmetics. However, in addition to these duties, the FDA is responsible for ensuring that most foods and beverages in the United States—including those that come from overseas—are accurately labeled and safe to eat and drink. The agency sets broad operating and safety standards for about 80 percent of the food and drink products bought and consumed by Americans.

The FDA's main food safety division is the Center for Food Safety and Applied Nutrition (CFSAN). Products regulated by CFSAN include fruits and vegetables, dairy products, seafood, processed foods, and food additives such as artificial coloring. Foods that are not regulated by CFSAN include meat and poultry, which are the responsibility of the USDA. Labeling of alcoholic beverages falls to the Alcohol and Tobacco Tax and Trade Bureau (TTB), and responsibility for the quality of drinking water belongs to the EPA.

A Closer Look

A 2007 report by the FDA Science Board subcommittee on science and technology stated that inadequate funding combined with increased workloads caused top scientists to leave their jobs at the FDA. This staffing shortage left the agency unable to keep up with advances in science and continued globalization in the industries that fall under its responsibility.

The FDA and the USDA share responsibility for ensuring the safety of eggs. Finally, the FDA's Center for Veterinary Medicine (CVM) oversees the safety of animal feeds and drugs, including those used in the raising of pigs, cows, and other food-producing animals.

Despite the fact that the FDA is responsible for the safety of 80 percent of the U.S. food supply, it receives only about 40 percent of the federal government dollars devoted to food safety; most of the rest goes to the USDA. In 2018, the FDA employed about 1,000 people in CFSAN. According to the Congressional Research Service, these employees are responsible for overseeing the operations of more than 44,000 domestic food manufacturers; 100,000 grain elevators, food warehouses, and other facilities; and 200,000 foreign food facilities.

Due to budget shortfalls, the FDA has been unable to inspect these various facilities as frequently as it would like. FDA officials estimate that surprise inspections of U.S. food manufacturers only take place every five to ten years. They assure citizens, though, that "high-risk" facilities—those that have a record of food safety violations—are inspected much more frequently. Altogether, the HHS reports that the FDA inspects less than 30 percent of domestic food-manufacturing facilities each year.

Increasing its use of technology has helped the FDA make the most of its available employees. The 2011 FDA Food Safety Modernization Act implemented a plan to get ahead of potential risks of foodborne illness. The Reportable Foods Registry (RFR) is an online portal that food industry officials must use to report when they think their products might pose a risk to public safety. This allows the FDA to act quickly to dispatch inspectors for risk control reviews (RCRs), where the inspector determines how the risk that has been reported can be reduced or eliminated. In the 2018 fiscal year, the RFR was used to send inspectors to more than 200 facilities to conduct RCRs.

The Centers for Disease Control and Prevention

The HHS is also home to a second federal agency with critical food safety and security responsibilities. The Centers for Disease Control and Prevention (CDC) is the chief scientific investigator of foodborne illnesses in the United States. It works closely with local and state public health departments to identify and control foodborne pathogens responsible for outbreaks of disease. CDC laboratories also carry out ongoing

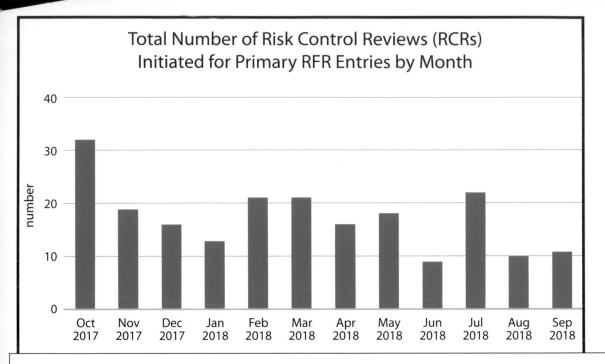

Total Number of Risk Control Reviews (RCRs) Initiated for Primary RFR Entries by Month

Considering how many food production sites exist, the number of risk assessments performed each month is relatively low, as this information from the FDA shows.

research into ways that food and beverage safety can be enhanced at all stages of production.

Over the years, the CDC has established several foodborne illness surveillance programs. The most prominent of these programs is FoodNet. First launched in 1996 in partnership with the USDA, FoodNet collects data on foodborne illness outbreaks across the United States. It includes research studies, physician and population surveys, and ongoing monitoring of microbiology laboratories that conduct tests on disease outbreaks. According to the Congressional Research Service, "FoodNet data allow CDC to have a clearer picture of the incidence and causes of foodborne illness and to establish baseline data against which to measure the success of changes in food safety programs."[14] In 2017, FoodNet laboratories received reports of more than 5,600 hospitalizations and 112 deaths related to various foodborne infections.

Another important CDC program is PulseNet, which acts as an early warning system for outbreaks of foodborne disease. The PulseNet

Superbugs

Antibiotics are medications that are used to treat bacterial infections, but overuse has led to bacteria that have evolved to become resistant to treatment with these drugs. These "superbugs" are difficult to treat and can spread rapidly through a population.

It is not just humans who are treated with antibiotics—the livestock that are used for food are routinely treated with antibiotics even when they do not show signs of illness. The antibiotics kill most of the bacteria in the animal's system, but the strongest bacteria survive. They multiply and spread to animal products, fruits and vegetables, and the rest of the environment, where people can come into contact with them and get sick. In the United States, an estimated 2 million people each year become infected with antibiotic-resistant bacteria.

The CDC has created strategies to prevent foodborne infections caused by superbugs. One of these strategies involves research into the genetic make-up of antibiotic-resistant bacteria to help identify the source of superbugs and patterns of how they may spread. The CDC also partners with veterinarians to ensure they have the tools and training to prescribe antibiotics to animals in a way that minimizes the risk of creating superbugs.

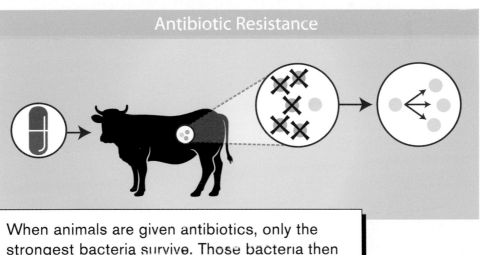

Antibiotic Resistance

When animals are given antibiotics, only the strongest bacteria survive. Those bacteria then breed other strong bacteria, creating superbugs.

program uses scientific "fingerprinting" of foodborne pathogens to determine bacterial strains that are genetically similar and therefore likely to have come from the same source. This process is known as whole genome sequencing. The organization uses this technology to alert state officials to take measures to prevent an outbreak. The CDC also maintains Epi-X, an internet-based communication tool that allows CDC officials, as well as state and local public health agencies, to access and share information on foodborne illnesses. OutbreakNet Enhanced is another web-based program that helps the CDC and local, state, and federal agencies cooperate with one another when investigating disease outbreaks due to foodborne bacteria and other causes.

The U.S. Department of Agriculture

The USDA is responsible for ensuring the safety of virtually all of the meat and poultry products that are consumed in American kitchens, cafeterias, and restaurants every day. In addition to its inspections and enforcement actions, the USDA has also served a historical function as a vocal supporter of the agriculture industry. The USDA's role as a marketing arm for U.S. farmers has undoubtedly helped American agriculture grow and prosper. This advertising function, however, has also led critics to accuse the agency of being "an apologist for bad decisions made by the food conglomerates" that "tailors its rules to satisfy industry more than to satisfy the needs of the taxpaying public."[15]

The USDA carries out most of its food safety duties through the Food Safety and Inspection Service (FSIS), which maintained a staff of about 9,600 people as of 2018. Most of these staff members are stationed at various plants across the United States, inspecting more than 3 billion pounds of meat, poultry, and egg products and performing about 190,000 scientific analyses every year. FSIS personnel are responsible for continuously monitoring whether these plants are meeting federal safety and sanitary standards. Some states choose to operate their own meat or poultry inspection programs, but even in these cases, the FSIS is responsible for overseeing the state programs to make sure that they are at least equal to the federal program.

Finally, the FSIS is responsible for certifying that imported meat and poultry products are safe for human consumption. Imported products that fall under the FSIS's responsibility range from popular meats that come from cows, pigs, and chickens to more unusual meat products from goats, geese, ostriches, quail, and guinea fowl.

In addition to the FSIS, the USDA includes several other agencies that play a role in protecting the nation's food supply. The Agricultural Research Service (ARS) performs food safety research that the FSIS incorporates into its inspection duties, while the Animal and Plant Health Inspection Service (APHIS) works to protect livestock and crops from diseases, insects, and mistreatment. The USDA's Food and Nutrition Service (FNS), meanwhile, coordinates efforts to make sure that school lunch programs are safe and nutritious for children.

A Closer Look

The FSIS Office of Public Health Science has three laboratory sites located in California, Georgia, and Missouri. Scientists employed there analyze products and environmental samples to study the four main microbial hazards: *E. coli*, *Salmonella*, *Campylobacter*, and *Listeria*.

Other Federal Regulators of Food Safety

Although the FDA and USDA act as the primary defenders of America's food supply at the federal level, a few other federal agencies also provide food security services at one point or another in the food supply chain. The best known of these agencies is the EPA. The EPA's Office of Prevention, Pesticides and Toxic Substances establishes legal tolerances, or limits, on the amount of pesticides that can be safely used on food crops. This affects not only the residue of dangerous chemicals left on food, but also runoff of those chemicals that might end up in the ground, in the air, and in the local water supply.

The Federal Trade Commission (FTC) is generally associated with consumer protection against unfair business practices, not food safety. As part of that larger mission, though, the FTC does enforce laws that forbid food companies from making misleading or outright false statements about their products. The National Marine Fisheries Service, meanwhile, offers voluntary seafood inspection programs to the fishing industry.

Empowering Young People

Each year, more than 6 million American children and teenagers participate in the USDA's respected 4-H program. First established in 1902, the 4-H program focused for many years on the nation's farming families. It became firmly associated in the minds of millions of children with county fairs, state fairs, and other events that celebrate America's agricultural heritage.

Over the years, though, 4-H has developed programs that serve suburban and city youth as well as those who live in farming and ranching communities. Some of these programs challenge 4-H youth to increase their skills in science, engineering, mathematics, animal science, and other subjects. Others encourage young adults to learn about important issues such as climate change and global food shortages. One of 4-H's most successful initiatives is its Food Safety and Quality Assurance (FSQA) program. This program helps young adults understand their role in producing safe and healthy food—and also helps them understand the importance of making wise and ethical decisions related to food production.

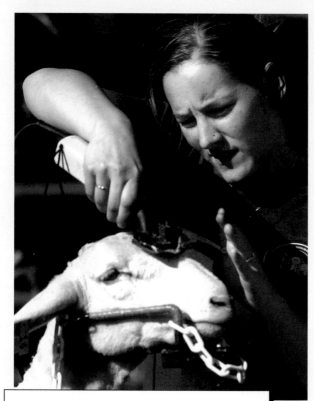

The 4-H program teaches young people about agriculture.

Finally, the Bureau of Alcohol, Tobacco, Firearms and Explosives (ATF) is responsible for enforcing laws and regulations relating to the manufacture, distribution, and use of alcoholic beverages. These regulations include extensive production and distribution guidelines to ensure the safety of beer, wine, and liquor.

Congressional Responsibilities

Numerous agencies within the federal government share responsibility for ensuring food security and safety in the United States. However, it is the U.S. Congress that makes the laws that give these agencies their authority and determines how much funding they receive to carry out their missions. Congress thus plays an enormous role in shaping food regulation and safety in the United States.

Any member of Congress, whether serving in the Senate or the House of Representatives, may introduce proposals for new laws governing food safety or any other policy area. After a bill has been introduced, it is assigned to a committee for review. In the House of Representatives, food safety bills go to one of the following committees for consideration: Agriculture; Energy and Commerce; Oversight and Government Reform; or Science, Space, and Technology. In the Senate, food safety policy is overseen by the Committee on Agriculture, Nutrition, and Forestry; the Committee on Health, Education, Labor, and Pensions; and the Committee on Homeland Security and Governmental Affairs. Historically, congressional committees devoted to food safety issues have been dominated by lawmakers from farm states—states that are heavily reliant on agriculture for their economic prosperity.

A bill can only go on for a vote in the full House or Senate if the assigned committee approves it. If a mutually satisfactory version passes both houses of Congress, it then goes to the president of the United States for their signature to become law.

Chapter Three

FOODBORNE GERMS THAT THREATEN AMERICA'S FOOD SUPPLY

Kevin Kowalcyk was a healthy two-year-old boy living in a small town outside Madison, Wisconsin. In the summer of 2001, he went on a vacation with his parents and older sister. The family enjoyed their road trip visiting friends and relatives and seeing sights such as the Baseball Hall of Fame, Plymouth Rock, and Niagara Falls.

On July 31, just two weeks after they returned home from their vacation, Kevin awoke during the night feeling sick. His parents were alarmed to see that he had diarrhea with blood in it, and they rushed him to the hospital. His condition worsened, and finally the family received the diagnosis: *E. coli* bacteria were making their small son very sick. In just days, Kevin's kidneys began to fail. Within seven days of his diagnosis, Kevin was heavily sedated and on a ventilator. "By the end of the week, he was receiving more medications than we could count to stabilize his blood pressure and heart rate. He had received eight units of blood,"[16] remembered Kevin's mother, Barbara. Tragically, the hospital care was not enough to save Kevin, and he died on August 11, 2001.

In the weeks after Kevin's death, his family followed up with their county's public health department, which had been notified of Kevin's diagnosis and had collected stool samples from the rest of the family while Kevin was in intensive care. They were shocked to learn that Kevin's father and sister had also tested positive for the same strain of *E. coli* that killed Kevin, though their symptoms had been barely noticeable. After losing her son, Barbara went on to earn a doctorate in environmental health with a focus on epidemiology—the study of the spread and control of disease—and now works as an advocate campaigning for better food safety on a national level.

The Threat of *E. Coli*

The *E. coli* germ that took Kevin's life is just one of several types of toxic bacteria that have been responsible for outbreaks of foodborne illness in the United States and around the world over the past few decades. It is probably the best known of these pathogens, however, since the most virulent strain of the bacterium, known as *E. coli* O157:H7, was the culprit in so many major outbreaks in the 1980s and 1990s.

E. coli strains have long been present in cows, other livestock, and humans, but until the early 1980s, the bacteria was relatively harmless to humans. Although people sometimes ate meat containing *E. coli*, human stomach acid was generally able to kill off the bacteria before it could do any damage. Beginning in the mid-20th century, however, cattle ranchers switched their livestock to a diet of corn, which made cow digestive systems more acidic than they had been when the animals were fed grass or hay. The switch gradually made *E. coli* more resistant to acid.

Around this same period, the *E. coli* strain O157:H7 took on a much more poisonous form when it interacted with a related toxic bacterium called *Shigella*. The result, wrote Paul Roberts, was a pathogen "that could withstand the acid shock of the human stomach and reach the intestine intact … Precisely when these adaptations occurred isn't known, but by 1982, when an outbreak of O157:H7 sickened forty-seven McDonald's customers, the bug's new weaponry was both fully formed and more lethal than anything investigators had ever seen."[17]

The *E. coli* germ typically escapes the digestive system of cows and contaminates meat during the slaughtering process. Humans get infections when they digest undercooked beef, although they can also get sick from water, milk, and other foods that have come into contact with *E. coli*–tainted meat or animal waste. In addition, *E. coli* bacteria have been known to be passed from person to person by contact, especially in crowded places such as nursing homes, schools, and day care centers.

Symptoms of *E. coli* generally appear within seven days of infection. The most common signs include severe abdominal cramps and severe or bloody diarrhea. Nausea and vomiting are also common, along with fatigue and fever. In many cases, people recover from an *E. coli* attack after a few days. However, some strains of *E. coli*, including O157:H7, produce the Shiga toxin, which attacks red blood cells and can cause kidney failure. This complication, which is known as hemolytic uremic

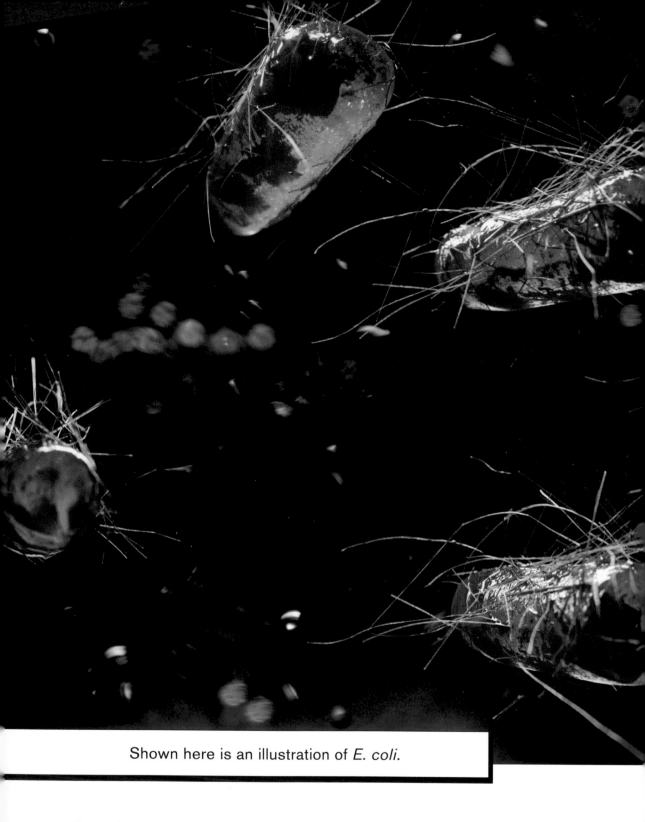

Shown here is an illustration of *E. coli*.

syndrome, is a particularly serious risk for children.

Outbreaks of foodborne sickness from *E. coli* O157:H7 have declined since 1994, when the U.S. government began classifying the strain as an adulterant. This measure forced the nation's beef industry to test for the presence of *E. coli* O157:H7 and take other safety precautions to guard against the bacteria. Nevertheless, the CDC estimates that O157:H7 and other Shiga toxin-producing *E. coli* (STEC) still account for 265,000 infections, 3,600 hospitalizations, and about 30 deaths annually across the United States.

Meanwhile, several other strains of *E. coli* bacteria that were not placed on the government's adulterant list became significant public health threats as well during the 1990s and 2000s. By 2010, in fact, the CDC estimated that "non-O157" strains of *E. coli* accounted for twice the number of illnesses as *E. coli* O157:H7. In 2011, the USDA finally added six other *E. coli* strains—O26, O45, O103, O111, O121, and O145—to the list of adulterants for which meat processors must test.

Salmonella: A Deadly Threat

Salmonella is another bacterium that has infiltrated America's food supply. This pathogen, in fact, now ranks as the country's deadliest source of foodborne illness. According to the CDC, foodborne salmonellosis strikes 1.2 million Americans every year. Of these cases, about 23,000 victims require hospitalization. Public health experts also blame salmonellosis for about 450 deaths every year. Nonetheless, the food industry has managed to keep the U.S. government from classifying *Salmonella* as an adulterant—a change that would force food producers to spend more money on testing and other safety measures.

Salmonella bacteria live in the intestinal tracts of humans and many other animals, including birds, livestock, and pets. Most cases of salmonellosis occur when people eat food that is contaminated with animal feces. This contamination generally occurs during food processing, but it can also take place if an infected person handles food with unwashed hands. Contamination can also occur when juices from raw, *Salmonella*-tainted meat or poultry make contact with vegetables, fruits, and other ready-to-eat foods. This is why experts recommend never using the same knife to cut both raw meat and produce.

The symptoms of salmonellosis generally include some combination of fever, diarrhea, and stomach cramps within 72 hours of eating the contaminated food. Some people also experience chills, headache, nausea, and vomiting. People typically recover from salmonellosis within four to seven days. However, for people with immune systems that are weakened or not fully developed, this illness is much more serious. Infants and young children; pregnant women and their unborn babies; elderly adults; and people with cancer, diabetes, HIV/AIDS, and other medical conditions that affect the immune system all have an increased risk of dying from salmonellosis.

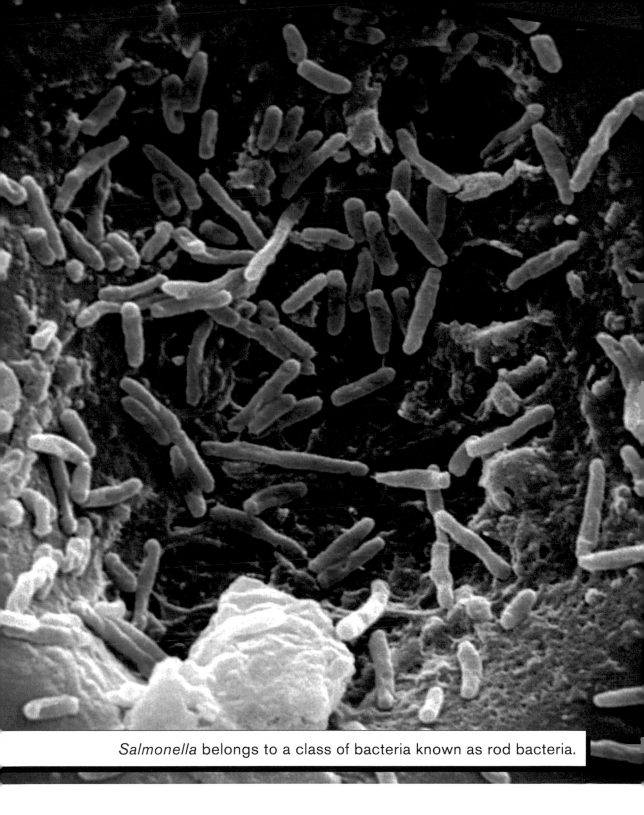

Salmonella belongs to a class of bacteria known as rod bacteria.

Estimating Cases of Foodborne Illness

Public health authorities and scientific research agencies such as the CDC work very hard to figure out how often Americans become sick from foodborne pathogens. Researchers admit that determining the exact number of people who are sickened from foodborne microbes is virtually impossible because many cases go unreported. In other instances, people who become sick from contaminated food assume that they are simply suffering from the flu or some other non-food-related bug.

Nonetheless, food safety researchers have become much more skilled at calculating rates of foodborne illness since the late 1970s, when they first began undertaking such studies. Today's scientists use sophisticated surveys, hospital records, and many other data sources to make their estimates. In addition, the 2010 FDA Food Safety Modernization Act included provisions to increase food safety testing and data collection efforts across the country.

Norovirus: The Biggest Hazard in Food Safety

Although disease outbreaks from *Salmonella* and *E. coli* bacteria are fairly common, they are still rare compared to norovirus, also called the stomach flu. This family of related viruses is the leading cause of foodborne disease outbreaks in the United States. The CDC estimated in 2018 that about 20 million Americans contract norovirus every year and that norovirus accounts for about 58 percent of all foodborne illness in the United States—more than all other foodborne bacteria, viruses, and parasites combined.

Fortunately, norovirus does not tend to make people as ill as some other foodborne pathogens do. People generally recover from norovirus infections within a day or two of medical treatment. Still, the CDC reports that 56,000 to 71,000 norovirus victims require hospitalization every year—and that between 570 and 800 Americans die from norovirus annually. As with other foodborne pathogens, norovirus frequently takes a heavier toll on young children, senior citizens, and people who are already in poor health.

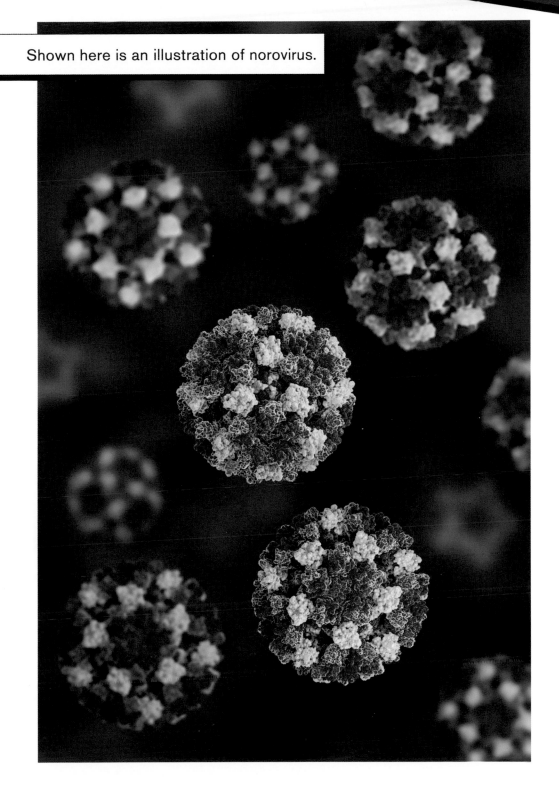

Shown here is an illustration of norovirus.

Where Do Norovirus Outbreaks from Food Contamination Happen?

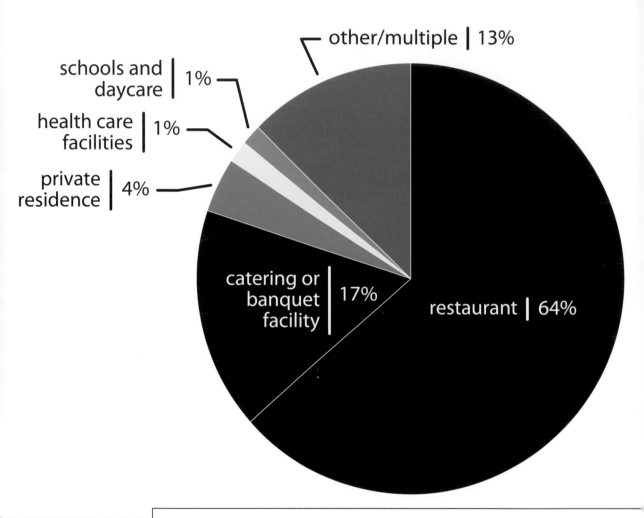

other/multiple | 13%

schools and daycare | 1%

health care facilities | 1%

private residence | 4%

catering or banquet facility | 17%

restaurant | 64%

Most foodborne norovirus outbreaks begin in restaurants, as this chart from the CDC shows.

People can contract norovirus from contaminated food or drink, touching objects that are contaminated with the virus, or direct contact with an already infected person. Symptoms of norovirus include nausea, vomiting, and diarrhea, and in some cases, infection can cause inflammation of the stomach and intestines, which is known as gastroenteritis.

The Threat of *Listeria*

Listeria is another foodborne pathogen that has become a dangerous presence in the American food supply. For example, a 2011 outbreak of *Listeria*-tainted cantaloupe killed 33 people across the country. This outbreak ranks as the second-deadliest epidemic of food poisoning in U.S. history. The CDC estimates that *Listeria* accounts for about 260 deaths every year in the United States, even though only about 1,600 cases are reported annually. This means that nearly one out of every six people who are afflicted with *Listeria* die from it.

Listeria bacteria are deadly because they are both hardy and hard-hitting. Unlike most bacteria, *Listeria* can grow and multiply in some foods under refrigerated conditions. In addition, *Listeria* germs have the ability to contaminate not only a wide variety of raw foods, such as uncooked meats and produce, but also cooked and processed foods such as soft cheeses, hot dogs, and packaged deli meats. Unpasteurized milk and milk products are at especially high risk for harboring *Listeria*.

Common symptoms of listeriosis include fever, muscle aches, and diarrhea. Other symptoms sometimes include headache, stiff neck, feelings of confusion, and problems with balance. Doctors and public health experts note, however, that the symptoms of listeriosis can vary significantly from person to person. It can be more difficult to trace than some other bacteria because it may not present symptoms for many weeks after the patient comes into contact with the germ.

Listeria is particularly dangerous for pregnant women. Although many expectant mothers experience little more than a touch of flu-like symptoms from the pathogen, listeriosis often spells serious trouble for the fetuses they carry. Infections during pregnancy can lead to miscarriage, stillbirth, premature delivery, or a life-threatening infection for a newborn. Pregnant women are also far more likely to contract listeriosis than the general population, so they must be even more careful with their food preparation. Other people at increased risk of death from *Listeria* include young children, elderly adults, and people with weakened immune systems.

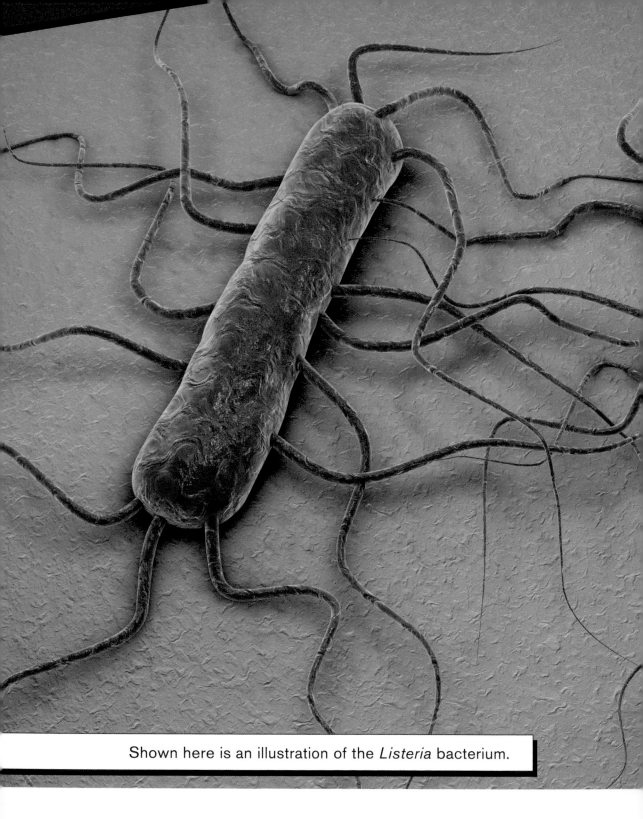

Shown here is an illustration of the *Listeria* bacterium.

Food and Water Contamination with *Campylobacter*

Another bacterium that is responsible for many cases of foodborne illness is *Campylobacter*. Cases of campylobacteriosis typically soar during the summer months, when warm conditions provide ideal breeding grounds for the bacteria. In addition, most cases of campylobacteriosis originate with raw or undercooked chicken, which is a popular summertime food for grilling. Chicken is a key vector for the spread of *Campylobacter* at all times of year, though. The bacteria are easily transmitted through the animals at chicken production facilities, and experts believe food producers have done a poor job of protecting chicken products from this type of contamination. In a 2014 study, the National Antimicrobial Resistance Monitoring System (NARMS) found *Campylobacter* in 33 percent of raw chicken samples from retailers.

The CDC estimated that the U.S. population experiences about 1.3 million cases of food poisoning from *Campylobacter* annually. However, unlike many other foodborne pathogens, *Campylobacter* generally does not cause full-blown outbreaks that sicken dozens or hundreds of people at a time. Instead, infection is generally confined to one person at a time, although *Campylobacter* outbreaks linked to contaminated water and unpasteurized milk have occurred in the past. Public health experts say that the rarity of *Campylobacter* outbreaks is due in part to the fact that the germ is very difficult to transmit directly from one person to another; it is almost always contracted directly from consumption of tainted food or drink. Public health experts have warned, however, that people with undeveloped or weakened immune systems are at special risk of infection.

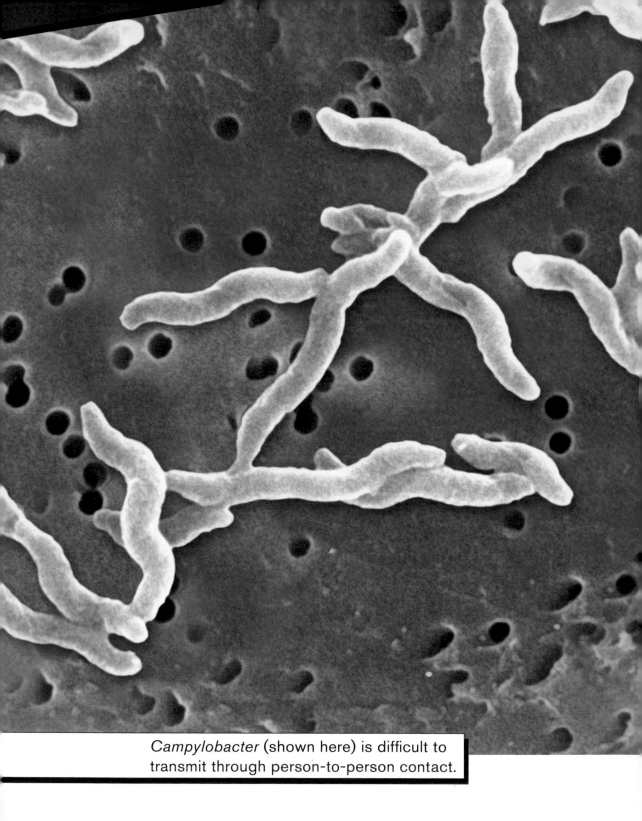

Campylobacter (shown here) is difficult to
transmit through person-to-person contact.

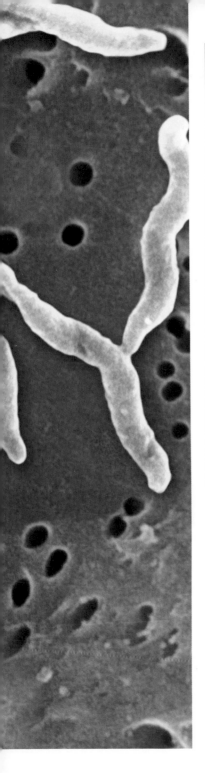

Finding the Culprit

When people get food poisoning, it is common for them to blame the last thing they ate. Sometimes this can result in restaurants or grocery stores being blamed for selling tainted food. However, experts note that because of the incubation period most pathogens require, people almost never show food poisoning symptoms immediately. The true culprit may actually be a food someone ate several days before getting sick.

Figuring out the cause of an illness is further complicated by the fact that many non-foodborne pathogens can cause the same symptoms as food poisoning. As the website Lifehacker pointed out, "Maybe you forgot to wash your hands after touching something covered in germs, like your phone or a railing, then ate some finger food … Stress, anxiety, anger, sadness, and other taxing things that weigh on your mind could [also] be what's causing the problem."[1]

1. Patrick Allan, "Stop Blaming Food Poisoning on the Last Thing You Ate," Lifehacker, July 6, 2017. lifehacker.com/stop-blaming-food-poisoning-on-the-last-thing-you-ate-1796688099.

Most people who contract campylobacteriosis begin to show symptoms within two to five days of exposure. Common symptoms include diarrhea that is sometimes bloody, fever, and stomach cramps. Nausea and vomiting also occur in some cases. Campylobacteriosis generally runs its course in about five to ten days. In rare cases, though, campylobacteriosis can cause a disease called Guillain-Barré syndrome (GBS). This rare disorder causes the victim's immune system to start attacking their nervous system, which in turn causes varying degrees of paralysis depending on how severe the person's case is. Most people eventually recover, but the timeline for recovery can range from a few weeks to several years.

Raw chicken often carries *Campylobacter*, so it is important for people to wash knives and cutting boards thoroughly after raw chicken has touched them.

The Ongoing Fight Against Disease

Everyone involved in food safety regulation in America recognizes that foodborne bacteria and viruses are always present. Scientists point out, in fact, that bacteria, viruses, fungi, and other microbes have always been—and will always remain—an important part of life on the planet. As food safety expert Marion Nestle explained,

> *Microbes are everywhere: around us, on us, and in us. They inhabit soil and water, skin and digestive tract, and any place that provides favorable conditions for growth ... Most are harmless, some are even "friendly," helping to make bread, wine, vinegar, soy sauce, yogurt, and cheese, and keeping our digestive tracts healthy. Others are less helpful; left to their own devices, they rot apples, mold bread, and spoil meat.* [18]

The challenge facing Americans and other people around the world is to take a firmer stand against the bacteria and viruses that can be harmful. The first key in defending against these pathogens is to appreciate just how tough they are. Food safety experts, public health officials, and agribusiness researchers all emphasize that the pathogens that dominate the headlines on cable TV news programs and news websites are naturally occurring bacteria that have a knack for taking advantage of any opportunity to spread and grow. Roberts noted that "food-borne pathogens, like all microbes, are quintessential adapters: they can modify their genetics, and thus

A Closer Look

The CDC has identified more than 250 different kinds of foodborne diseases.

their physical structure and behavior, to defend themselves against antibiotics and to exploit new opportunities."[19]

The second step in combating food contamination is to create and follow effective food safety regulations and policies. While it may not be possible to completely and irreversibly eliminate all pathogens from the public's food supply, common-sense safety measures can make a great deal of difference to people's health.

Chapter Four

REDUCING THE THREAT OF FOODBORNE PATHOGENS

The emergence of new technologies has allowed the United States to produce more food and to do it faster and cheaper than ever before. However, it has also led to conditions for food production that may create a danger to the health of the American public. Families in the 1970s did not spend a lot of time wondering if the food on their tables was safe to eat; food poisoning seemed like a rare threat. When they did become sick, the illness was rarely severe enough to report to the authorities. Since the 1970s, however, reports of food poisoning have increased.

In 2011, the CDC reported that roughly 48 million Americans—about one out of six people—get sick every year from foodborne diseases. The agency also reported that contaminated food and drink result in 128,000 hospitalizations and 3,000 deaths every year. Other studies, meanwhile, indicate that food-related sickness costs Americans billions of dollars annually in health care expenses, lost wages, and higher insurance costs. Media coverage of disastrous outbreaks has increased as well, raising awareness among Americans of the threat of contaminated food and causing lawmakers to act.

The Question of a Food Safety Crisis

The results of numerous scientific studies have spurred intense debate about the state of food safety in the United States. Some scientists, researchers, and consumer advocates believe that the nation is facing a full-blown crisis in food safety and that consumers should demand major improvements in industry practices. Activist Diane Carmen, for example, expressed disbelief after a 2002 recall of 19 million pounds of

People rarely think about food safety when they sit down to eat.

hamburger infected with *E. coli* failed to encourage any major new food safety regulations. "If 19 million pounds of meat distributed to half of this country had been contaminated with a deadly strain of *E. coli* bacteria by terrorists, we'd go nuts," she wrote. "But when it's done by a Fortune 100 corporation [ConAgra Foods], we continue to buy it and feed it to our kids."[20]

Other observers, though, question whether a crisis exists. The food industry as well as some independent researchers say that the threat of foodborne illness has been exaggerated. According to Terry Etherton, a professor of animal nutrition and animal science at Penn State University:

> *The story of how agricultural research and contemporary food production practices allow the United States to produce the world's*

safest food supply is one that tends to get "lost" in the media frenzy that explodes after a disease outbreak is linked to food. When one looks at the record of foodborne diseases throughout history, it is evident that we have an armada of scientific and public health resources today that are remarkably effective at reducing the risk of contracting disease from food.[21]

Despite such sentiments, however, public skepticism about the safety of the American food supply appears to be on the rise. Such doubts have generated renewed demands for additional food safety procedures and regulations. Government officials, consumer advocates, and members of the food industry have all responded to these calls for reform by proposing new—and very different—ideas to better ensure U.S. food security.

Taking Precautions at Home

The big corporations that dominate America's food industry emphasize that food safety can be dramatically improved if consumers follow a few simple rules, since even the cleanest food is subject to infection by pathogens if proper precautions are not taken during preparation. These precautions include making sure meat and egg dishes are cooked to the proper internal temperature so potentially dangerous bacteria are killed by the high heat. Other food safety suggestions include washing hands frequently when handling food and thoroughly washing ready-to-serve fruits and vegetables before eating. Even produce such as oranges and avocados should be washed before peeling, since germs on the outside can transfer to the part that is eaten as the rind is removed. Keeping certain foods cold and keeping track of how long foods, especially meat products, have been in the refrigerator is another important precaution everyone should take. Some foods spoil in as little as two hours, especially if they are left out on a counter, and spoiled foods are breeding grounds for foodborne pathogens even if they were not infected when they were bought. In the event of a power outage, keeping the freezer and refrigerator doors closed as much as possible is the best way to prevent the food inside from getting warm enough to spoil. After 24 hours without power, the foods inside should be thrown away.

Washing fruits and vegetables is one good way to prevent the spread of foodborne illnesses.

Consumers can also use common-sense approaches to shopping. For example, many people enjoy going to farmers' markets, where local farmers bring produce, animal meat, and other food products to sell. Knowing exactly where their food is coming from makes many people feel more secure, but the food at these markets is not immune to picking up pathogens. When selecting food from a farmers' market, there are several things shoppers should do, according to Amanda Deering, a clinical assistant professor at Purdue University's Food Science Department and a trainer for Safe Produce Indiana:

- Ask the seller exactly where the food is coming from if there is no sign displayed.
- Inquire about the growing process and what types of pesticides, if any, have been used.
- Check if the food is properly displayed—for example, whether the booth has a cover over it and whether all the food is out of reach of dogs and other animals.
- Check if a lot of people are handling the food that is for sale, and, if possible, ask for items that have not yet been touched by many people.

These precautions are sensible and effective in limiting exposure to foodborne pathogens. However, public health experts and safe-food advocates point out that it is also in agribusiness's self-interest to push these sorts of consumer-oriented solutions. By emphasizing the benefits of proper cooking and handling of food by consumers, corporations at various points along the food pipeline can avoid new safety regulations that decrease their profits. "Maintaining food safety is a cost," wrote food safety advocate Tom Philpott, "and the temptation exists to cut corners."[22]

Many experts note that although it is important for consumers to take precautions when handling their own food, there are other considerations to take into account. One is that many consumers who do prepare their own food are not fully aware of proper cooking and food handling precautions. This has led to a push for easily accessible food safety campaigns and classes. Another is that American food consumers have no control over food handling and preparation techniques when they go out to eat—and food safety violations can happen in any restaurant kitchen, no matter how upscale it is.

In February 2019, the *Mercury*—the campus newspaper for the University of Texas at Dallas—published an article claiming that many of the on-campus food service workers had not received food safety training within 60 days of being hired, as Texas state law requires. In this job, as in many food service jobs, training is done through fellow employees who have been there longer. This means not everyone receives the same quality of training. The likelihood of this scenario increases in places with high turnover rates, meaning people frequently find new jobs and are replaced by newer workers. With so many new employees coming in, managers may find it difficult to schedule time to train them, and with other things to think about, the training may eventually be completely forgotten. Some companies also place other considerations ahead of food safety. For example, employees who handle food should not come to work when they are sick, but many food service employers do not give their workers sick days and employees may not be able to afford to be out of work for several days. This situation is made worse when companies expect perfect or near-perfect attendance and threaten to fire workers who are not able to come in when they are scheduled.

Farming Animals and Breeding Diseases

Much of the criticism of America's food safety focuses on the big meat-production operations that dominate the beef, pork, and poultry industries. These operations, which are known as CAFOs or "factory farms," house huge numbers of animals in extremely close quarters. These systems enable factory farms to produce large quantities of meat, dairy products, and eggs very inexpensively. However, they have also become major breeding grounds for foodborne pathogens such as *E. coli*, *Salmonella*, and *Campylobacter*.

The main problem is that livestock crowded into these warehouses pass germs back and forth. A 2018 study by researchers at Cornell

Many people have protested the close living quarters animals endure on factory farms.

University College of Veterinary Medicine found that water troughs on farms are a major factor in the spread of *E. coli*. According to Renata Ivanek, the paper's senior author, "Water troughs appeared in our mathematical model as a place where water can get contaminated and a potential place where we could break the cycle."[23] Although more research is necessary to confirm these findings, preventing contamination of water troughs could provide farms with a low-cost way to stop pathogens from entering the food supply.

Preventing the spread of bacteria is preferable to treating cows with antibiotics because of the problem of bacterial resistance. The livestock industry makes heavy use of antibiotics to control disease in their tightly packed animal populations. Over time, however, the repeated doses of medicine have had the unintended side effect of creating new bacterial strains of *Salmonella*, *Campylobacter*, and other foodborne pathogens that are harder to kill with antibiotics. "With widespread use ... antibiotics became less effective because bacteria develop tools to resist them," explained one food safety study sponsored by the Center for Science in the Public Interest. "Antibiotics can wipe out most bacteria in a population, but the ones that survive have natural resistance. They reproduce and multiply, and soon the antibiotic has become useless in treating the disease."[24]

Many different proposals for reforming CAFOs—which have also been criticized for being cruel to animals and polluting rivers and lakes—have been made over the years. Consumer advocates, environmentalists, and public health professionals have all urged the passage of new regulations that would limit the size of these facilities, limit their use of antibiotics, and force them to implement new food safety technologies. All of these proposals have been met with opposition from the meat and dairy industries.

Does Irradiation Make Food Safer?

Meatpackers and fast-food companies claim that one of the best ways to reduce sickness from bacteria-tainted meat is through irradiation of meat products. This technology, which has been approved by organizations ranging from the American Medical Association (AMA) to the World Health Organization (WHO), involves treating raw food products with ionizing radiation that kills bacteria and parasites that would otherwise cause foodborne disease. It can also extend the shelf life of certain foods. According to the CDC, irradiation technology "holds great potential for preventing many important foodborne diseases that are transmitted through meat, poultry, fresh produce, and other foods."[25] Studies conducted by WHO, the International Atomic Energy Agency (IAEA), and the United Nations' Food and Agricultural Organization (FAO) have concluded with great certainty that this process does not decrease the nutritional value of the food or make it unsafe to eat. However, few national governments have approved the use of irradiated food, and some consumer advocacy and environmental groups within the United States strongly oppose irradiation as an industry practice.

Critics say that irradiated meats and other foods lose some of their nutritional value and do not taste as good as foods that have not been treated using this technology. They also worry that if meatpacking companies become dependent on irradiation technology to kill off dangerous pathogens, they will lose all incentive to maintain clean operations and keep animal waste and other contaminants out of the food supply. As one food industry journalist put it, "I don't want to be served irradiated feces along with my meat."[26]

A Closer Look

In 2002, the USDA approved the use of irradiated meat products in the nation's school lunch programs.

The FDA requires meat products in the United States that have undergone irradiation to be clearly identified with a radiation label if they are sold in stores, although food services and restaurants are not obligated to provide this information about the food they serve. Since many American consumers see "radiation" as a vaguely scary word, this labeling requirement has severely limited the use of irradiation in the meat industry. Meatpackers have tried to get the FDA to end the labeling requirement. Thus far, however, consumer advocates and other opponents of irradiation have managed to keep the FDA rule in place.

The Agriculture Industry's Influence Over Food Policies

Although agribusiness has so far been unsuccessful in its efforts to weaken or remove irradiation labeling requirements, food safety advocates believe that the industry holds a lot of influence over state and national food policies. They complain that powerful farming, food-processing, grocery, and restaurant groups have made massive campaign contributions to members of Congress in an effort to derail reforms that might have improved food safety. They point out, for example, that the USDA still does not require the meat industry to test for *Salmonella*, *Listeria*, *Campylobacter*, or any foodborne pathogens besides *E. coli* in their products, despite repeated calls from scientists and food safety advocates. "The main thrust of the industry is profits," explained one retired USDA veterinarian. "You can't add to profits by taking the time to run tests on a product."[27]

The heavy presence of former food industry executives in important government positions has also drawn criticism. "Food companies and trade groups ... have achieved a remarkable degree of influence in the ways that governors and presidents appoint the regulatory officials who oversee the food industry," wrote Paul Roberts, "with the result that top-echelon [high-ranking] officials at agencies like the USDA and the FDA often come straight from the ranks of the same food industries those agencies are supposed to regulate."[28]

In September 2010, the Union of Concerned Scientists and Iowa State University released the results of a survey of 1,700 employees in the FDA and the USDA. More than 620 respondents to the survey— 38 percent of the total—agreed or strongly agreed that "public health has been harmed by agency practices that defer to business interests."[29] More than 300 respondents (25 percent) stated that they personally knew of cases in the previous year where the food industry forced their agency to withdraw or significantly modify a policy or action designed to protect consumers from contaminated food. "Upper level management does not adequately support field inspectors and the actions they take to protect the food supply," said Dean Wyatt, who manages the USDA's slaughterhouse inspectors. "Not only is there lack of support, but there's outright obstruction, retaliation, and abuse of power."[30]

Steps to Improve Food Safety

Advocates for food safety reform admit that the food industry's strong political influence and large size complicate efforts to reduce foodborne illness. They emphasize, however, that even narrowly focused changes to America's vast food delivery system have the capacity to dramatically improve food safety.

For example, regulators and consumer advocates have long argued that outbreaks of foodborne illness could be greatly reduced   both in terms of their number and their severity—if it were easier to keep track of exactly where food comes from. "The fact that one cow's trimmings can impact hundreds of thousands—or even millions—of pounds of meat is a wake-up call,"[31] wrote journalist Ezra Klein.

Food safety advocates also say that the United States needs to do a better job of inspecting foods imported from other countries. A 2017 study by the CDC examining foodborne disease between 1996 and 2014 found that a total of 195 outbreaks resulting in 19 deaths were caused by foods that had been imported to the United States. Although nearly all of these outbreaks involved foods that are under the jurisdiction

Families Fighting for Food Safety Justice

In 1993, at a family cookout, Nancy Donley's six-year-old son Thomas ate a hamburger that was contaminated with *E. coli* O157:H7. Despite the best efforts of medical personnel, the young boy fell into a coma and died in a Chicago hospital.

The death of her child devastated Nancy and awakened her to the threat of foodborne pathogens in America's food supply. For this reason, she joined with other parents whose children had become sick or died from contaminated food to form Safe Tables Our Priority (STOP), an organization dedicated to establishing stronger food safety laws in the United States. The organization later changed its name to Stop Foodborne Illness. "My involvement is in dedication to Alex, who wanted to be a paramedic when he grew up so that 'I can help others,'"[1] Nancy explained.

1. Quoted in Warren Leon and Caroline Smith DeWaal, *Is Our Food Safe?: A Consumer's Guide to Protecting Your Health and the Environment.* New York, NY: Three Rivers Press, 2002, p. 24.

A single package of ground beef could contain parts from hundreds of individual animals.

of the FDA, the FDA examines only a very small portion of imported food shipments— less than 2 percent, by some estimates. This inattention poses a potentially lethal problem for American consumers, as the number of reported outbreaks from imported foods increased steadily over the years, according to this study.

A Closer Look

In August 1997, the meat-processing company Hudson Foods announced a recall of 25 million pounds of ground beef that had been tainted with *E. coli* at one of its facilities. That is enough meat, according to journalist Eric Schlosser, to provide every American with a tainted fast-food hamburger.

The Food Safety Modernization Act of 2011

Consumer advocates and officials at the FDA and USDA say that America's food safety system could be greatly strengthened if federal and state food safety agencies received more funding to hire more researchers and inspectors. They point out that the number of food inspectors in the USDA and FDA fell steadily during the 1980s and 1990s, which meant a decline in food safety inspections as well. The number of USDA employees responsible for monitoring food safety in the meat and poultry industries, for example, fell from 12,000 in 1978 to 7,500 in 1997. This

President Barack Obama signed into law the first comprehensive food safety reform in more than 70 years.

level of staffing has remained fairly constant ever since, even as mass food poisonings from *Salmonella*, *Listeria*, and *E. coli* continue to make news headlines.

In 2011, the FDA Food Safety Modernization Act (FSMA) was signed into law by President Barack Obama, paving the way to hire as many as 2,000 new FDA inspectors. Many consumer advocates, food experts, and FDA employees, though, believe that the act's other features will have an even greater impact on food safety. For the first time ever, the law gives the FDA the power to order recalls of contaminated foods. Before, food companies could decide for themselves whether to issue product recalls. It also requires farming operations and food-processing facilities to implement new food safety plans, and it gives the FDA access to internal records at farms and food-production facilities. In addition, the law requires importers to verify that food products grown or processed overseas meet all U.S. safety standards. As the Safe Food Alliance explained, "FSMA shifts the

Should a Single Federal Agency Be in Charge of Food Safety?

Under the current U.S. system, government responsibilities for food safety are divided among multiple agencies. Many critics claim that this system is confusing and inefficient. Some food safety advocates have argued that the U.S. government could more effectively manage its food safety obligations if it moved all of the food-related work of the USDA, FDA, EPA, and other departments into a single federal agency. Supporters of a single federal Department of Food say that establishing such an agency would make it much easier for the food industry to understand and obey food safety regulations. Even more importantly, such an agency might dramatically improve the safety of the foods and drinks that Americans consume every day. "A single agency would be able to develop transparent safety standards, consolidate and prioritize food safety programs, and coordinate the federal response to outbreaks of food contamination,"[1] said Jaydee Hanson, a policy analyst at the public health advocacy group Center for Food Safety.

1. Jaydee Hanson, "Do We Need a Department of Food?," *Room for Debate*, February 8, 2009. roomfordebate.blogs.nytimes.com/2009/02/08/do-we-need-a-department-of-food/.

focus of the FDA to ensuring food safety through prevention of microbial contamination rather than just reacting to the problem after it has already occurred."[32] In the years since the law was passed, the FDA has worked to put new policies in place to fulfill the law's requirements. Companies were given until January 2018 to be in compliance with most of the new policies and until January 2020 to be in compliance with certain rules regarding their water supply.

However, even supporters of the FSMA admit that the law is not perfect. For one thing, it does not include food safety provisions for the meat and poultry industries, which remain under the supervision of the USDA. Public health experts believe, though, that the law represents a welcome change in America's food safety priorities.

THE FOOD TECHNOLOGIES OF THE FUTURE

The increase in troublesome news headlines about foodborne illnesses and new scientific procedures that have not been in place long enough to give researchers long-term data have filled many Americans with a sense of foreboding about the safety of the food on their tables. Public health experts and doctors are keeping a close eye on trends in American health as advances in food science sweep through the industry. As companies work to meet increased demand for certain foods, scientists are measuring the side effects of the techniques of increased production.

Are Pesticides Safe to Use?

Food growers in the United States and other countries make extensive use of pesticides to protect their crops from harmful insects during the growing and harvest seasons, as well as during the storage and transportation phases. Pesticides allow farmers to increase the amount of usable food they can raise, and these chemicals can improve the quality, safety, and shelf life of certain foods.

The EPA regulates the use of pesticides, including chemicals that kill crop-destroying bugs (insecticides), weeds and other vegetation threats (herbicides), and damaging fungi (fungicides). Before a pesticide can be sold in the United States, it must first pass a set of tests to determine whether it is safe. Restrictions are imposed on different pesticides and are listed under the directions for use of that pesticide. The EPA considers the toxicity of the chemical ingredients, how much is applied and how often, and how much residue will remain on food by the time it is sold and prepared. These restrictions are designed to keep growers

Pesticide use is a controversial topic. Some people are less concerned about the effects pesticides may have on people who eat treated food than about the health effects on farmers who have to breathe those chemicals in as they spray them.

from using pesticides to the point that they actually make the food unhealthy or dangerous to eat. Nonetheless, some observers believe that current limitations—also known as tolerances—for pesticide residues on food crops and cattle feed are too high.

Most critics who say that there is too much pesticide residue in the food supply admit that individual strawberries, carrots, grapes, apples, peaches, corn, and other crops contain very little residue. The problem, say some public health and environmental groups, is that regulatory agencies have not sufficiently researched the health impact of ingesting pesticide residues over a long period of time. Food safety organizations such as the Pesticide Action Network also point out that the "EPA sets limits on the maximum amount of each pesticide that can be on each food item, but there's no limit to the number of different pesticides that can be on your food."[33]

Families that are worried about pesticides in their food have several options to reduce their exposure. Food safety advocates say that thoroughly washing and peeling fruits and vegetables can get rid of a lot of pesticide residue. In addition, food safety experts such as Warren Leon and Caroline Smith DeWaal noted that "choosing foods with little or no pesticide residues is getting easier and easier as organic products boasting a new national [USDA organic] label arrive at your local market ... Many parents can significantly reduce their children's pesticide exposure by switching to organically grown apples, peaches, and strawberries."[34]

However, organic food is more expensive, and not everyone can afford it. Medical professionals and food safety advocates agree that adults and

Some people believe organic produce is better to eat because it is grown without the use of pesticides. Others do not believe organic food's benefits justify the higher price tag.

children alike should still eat plenty of fruits and vegetables whether or not they are organic, and most organizations note that there is no evidence that organic foods have a higher nutritional content than non-organic ones. The Environmental Working Group (EWG) is an organization that is devoted to reducing pesticide levels in the food supply. The group firmly states that "All research agrees on the health benefits of a diet that includes fruits and vegetables, and eating fresh produce—organic or conventional, as budget allows—is essential for health."[35]

A Closer Look

In 2017, the CDC found residue of more than 300 environmental chemicals in samples of human blood, urine, breast milk, and other bodily fluids.

Dairy Hormones and Early Puberty

During the 1980s and 1990s, doctors, parents, scientists, and food safety advocates became tangled in a heated debate that is still ongoing today. The debate centers on whether consuming a lot of milk and certain other foods are partly responsible for the rise in "precocious puberty"—a phenomenon in which children enter puberty at an unusually early age.

There is widespread agreement about some of the factors that are contributing to this trend, which is also sometimes called early-onset puberty. Rising rates of obesity (one of the factors that triggers puberty is when a person reaches a certain weight), declining rates of exercise, and exposure to industrial chemicals such as those used in plastics manufacturing are all responsible to some degree for the rising percentage of children who are entering puberty at an early age—as young as six or seven in some cases. This is an important area of study because early puberty is associated with negative risk factors, such as anxiety, eating disorders, and substance abuse.

Some people believe that earlier puberty can also be linked to when the dairy industry began using artificial growth hormones in their cows

Many dairy products—including cheese, cream, and yogurt—are made with milk that comes from cows that have been treated with growth hormones.

in the mid-1990s. According to this theory, traces of those growth hormones are being passed along to children and teens through milk and other dairy products. Some people believe meat that contains growth hormones is also part of the problem. This theory has been widely discussed in all sorts of media, from environmental and public health magazines to parenting websites. In some cases, the link between early puberty and dairy products has been prematurely described as a scientifically proven one.

However, many researchers doubt any link exists between the consumption of hormone-laced dairy products and early puberty. Scientists say that milk-boosting hormones given to cows are mostly destroyed when their milk is pasteurized, and any that remain are destroyed during human digestion. Researchers also note that governments that forbid the use of growth hormones in their dairy herds,

"Dirty" versus "Clean" Produce

Each year, the EWG releases a study of pesticide contamination of popular fruits and vegetables sold in the United States. The organization publishes the "dirty dozen" list of fruits and vegetables found to be most contaminated by pesticides as well as a "clean fifteen" list of produce found to have the smallest traces of pesticides. As of 2019, the dirty dozen included strawberries, spinach, kale, nectarines, apples, grapes, peaches, cherries, pears, tomatoes, celery, and potatoes. The clean fifteen included avocados, sweet corn, pineapples, frozen sweet peas, onions, papayas, eggplants, asparagus, kiwis, cabbage, cauliflower, cantaloupes, broccoli, mushrooms, and honeydew melons.

In 2019, the USDA tested thousands of samples of produce and found a total of 225 different pesticides present. Related research conducted by the Harvard University EARTH group in 2018 found evidence linking the consumption of high-pesticide residue foods and fertility problems in women.

Cherries are among the produce that is most likely to contain pesticides.

such as Canada and countries in the European Union (EU), are seeing the same rise in early-onset puberty that the United States is experiencing. Finally, tests conducted by the FDA have concluded that there is no difference between milk produced by cows treated with growth hormones and those not treated with growth hormones.

The GM Debate

Even the controversies over pesticides and artificial growth hormones have been overshadowed by yet another debate about the role of modern technology and science in the raising of food. The issue in question concerns the manipulation of genes—the building blocks of all life—to create new varieties of crops that grow more quickly, yield more food, stay fresh longer, or naturally repel insects and mold. This high-tech food-growing method is variously known as genetic modification, bioengineering, and transgenic technology. However it is labeled, though, the practice has sharply divided consumers, scientists, environmental and public health organizations, and dietary experts.

Genetically modified (GM) foods have been sold commercially in the United States since 1992, when the FDA determined that GM products should be treated no differently than those produced by traditional farming methods. "The key factors in reviewing safety concerns [about food]," announced the FDA, "should be the characteristics of the food product, rather than the fact that the new methods are used."[36] Many environmental groups, consumer advocates, and scientists harshly condemned this ruling, arguing that bioengineered food was too new to predict what its long-term health effects would be.

By the mid-1990s, farmers all across the country were raising fields full of bioengineered corn, soybeans, and other crops. GM foods have increased in popularity ever since. By 2011, around 90 percent of America's corn and soybeans were produced from GM seeds. Many other U.S. fruits and vegetables, as well as non-food crops such as cotton, are now commonly produced through bioengineering as well. In 2011, federal authorities estimated that 60 to 70 percent of all processed foods on supermarket shelves contained genetically engineered ingredients.

American farmers are not the only ones using GM seeds either. Some nations, such as Canada, Japan, and many countries of the EU, have passed strict laws against bioengineered foods. Others,

More than 90 percent of the soybeans used to make nearly every packaged soy product available at the grocery store have been genetically modified.

however, have embraced the technology. By 2016, GM crops were being cultivated in 26 countries by more than 18 million farmers. Most of these farmers, wrote British politician and GM foods supporter Dick Taverne, "are resource-poor farmers in developing countries, mainly India and China. Most of these small-scale farmers grow pest-resistant GM cotton ... This cotton benefits farmers because it reduces the need for insecticides, thereby increasing their income and also improving their health."[37]

A Closer Look

According to a 2015 study by the Associated Press, 66 percent of Americans are in favor of requiring food manufacturers to label products that contain genetically modified ingredients.

Support for GM Foods

Supporters say that GM foods have benefits that can make the world a healthier and better place. Advocates frequently claim that the technology could prove essential in feeding an increasingly overpopulated planet because GM seeds produce much larger volumes of food than non-GM seeds. This means farmers can generate much more food without expanding the size of their fields or increasing their use of pesticides. In addition, researchers are working on GM crops that can grow in dry or cold environments. Such crops would be a great help to nations that have a limited supply of good farmland.

Another promising avenue of research lies in the development of foods that are genetically designed to carry extra health benefits. GM supporters say that this technology has the capacity to pack extra vitamins and nutrients into bananas, rice, spinach, and other foods. Such products could improve the health and vitality not only of American children and adults, but also of people around the world who have limited access to nutritious food.

Finally, advocates of food bioengineering claim that the technology has many environmental benefits. For example, some pest-resistant GM crops do not require as much spraying with herbicides or insecticides, which can pollute rivers, lakes, and groundwater resources. In addition, the high yields associated with GM crops have the potential to benefit natural ecosystems that support wildlife by reducing the amount of land needed for farming.

Concerns Over GM Foods

Most opponents of transgenic technology acknowledge that GM foods have some attractive features. They feel, however, that the potential drawbacks far outweigh the benefits. They also insist that it is much too early to predict what all of those drawbacks may be.

GM opponents believe that the rise of transgenic crops poses a number of potential threats to the environment. They worry that the genes contained in "mutant" foods will intermingle with and eventually destroy naturally occurring species of fruits and vegetables—as well as the animal species that depend on them. In addition, critics assert that some GM crops have unintended side effects on certain animals. There have been claims, for example, that pollen from transgenic corn has contributed to the decline in America's endangered monarch butterfly population, although these claims were discredited.

Most of the criticisms of GM foods, though, center on human health factors. Many critics believe that new bioengineered strains of food might cause new food allergies. "The government does not require biotechnology companies to test for allergens, and they rarely do," wrote

Pesticides in the Air

Many people worry about health threats from food laced with pesticides. People can also become ill, however, from absorbing pesticide residue through their skin. In eastern Washington, middle school student Elena Dominguez began suffering from a variety of mysterious health ailments, including seizures and fainting spells. Her mother, Cindy, suspected that her daughter's difficulties might have been due to pesticides that were being sprayed on apple orchards next to her school. Cindy contacted the USDA with her concerns, and agency investigators later found pesticide residue on Elena's gym clothes as well as the school playground and track field. The investigators and Elena's doctors decided that she was a victim of pesticide poisoning.

"I was relieved to finally get an answer," said Cindy, who from that point on made sure that her children stayed indoors when local orchards did their pesticide spraying. "But my neighbors' kids were still out there."[1] When Cindy first asked the school district to adopt policies to protect school children from drifting pesticide residues, she was ignored. However, when she threatened to take legal action, the school district took notice. Administrators secured a promise from the neighboring orchard owners to inform the school whenever they were planning a pesticide treatment so the school could keep kids inside.

1. Quoted in Ariana Kelly, "One Mom's Story About Pesticide Drift Near Schools," Moms Rising, February 18, 2010. www.momsrising.org/ blog/one-moms-story-about-pesticide-drift-near-schools/.

When pesticides are sprayed on crops, they drift into the air and can end up in people's lungs and on their skin.

Marion Nestle. "For one thing, testing is difficult. For another, testing is hardly in a company's best interest … Like testing for microbial pathogens, testing for allergens is risky: you might find one."[38] Discovering that information could potentially cost a company millions of dollars, as it would no longer be able to sell that food product.

Other complaints about the growing presence of GM products in the food supply focus on potential health problems that have yet to reveal themselves. Critics argue that experts do not yet know whether eating GM foods might cause health problems in the next century. For this reason, anti-GM groups and researchers have continually called on Congress, the FDA, and the USDA to monitor the industry much more closely and insist on higher levels of testing.

Lab-Grown Meat

Starting around 2009, several technology companies began producing meat products without killing animals. The so-called "clean meat," or cultured meat, is created from a tiny sample of muscle tissue from a living animal such as a cow. Scientists extract stem cells from the tissue and encourage them to grow into muscle cells, which multiply to form muscle fibers and eventually become a piece of beef. Companies such as Memphis Meats, Mosa Meat, and Finless Foods say that producing "meat without murder" can drastically improve their ability to feed millions of hungry people without relying on cruel and unsanitary factory farm conditions.

However, before clean meat can become widely available to the public, there are several barriers it must overcome. The first is cost. The process is currently prohibitively expensive, with a pound of lab-grown meat from Memphis Meats costing

Scientists are working to develop meat that can be grown in a lab. Supporters hope this could eliminate the crowded, unsanitary farming conditions that lead to the spread of foodborne pathogens.

around $2,400 in 2018. The second barrier is taste. The fat content of a hamburger has a significant impact on its flavor, so scientists formulating the lab-grown animal tissue must pay careful attention to content and texture.

The final—and perhaps largest—hurdle is public and governmental acceptance. According to Professor G. Owen Schaefer at the Center for Biomedical Ethics,

> To receive market approval, clean meat will have to be proved safe to eat. Although there is no reason to think that lab-produced meat would pose a health hazard, the FDA is only now beginning to consider how it should be regulated. Meanwhile traditional meat producers are pushing back, arguing that the lab-generated products are not meat at all and should not be labeled as such, and surveys show that the public has only tepid [unenthusiastic] interest in eating meat from labs.[39]

Despite these obstacles, clean meat companies are continuing their work and paving the way for a future where people might eat real meat that is produced in sanitary conditions without slaughter and that is as traceable as the lab that grew it.

Until that time, though, the majority of public interest is focusing on how to prevent outbreaks of foodborne illness using the tools that already exist. Fortunately, new breakthroughs are happening all the time. In February 2019, the Food Safety Authority of Ireland (FSAI) announced that it had a tool that can scan foods and identify their entire DNA content. This would be helpful in identifying foods that have not been properly labeled. According to *Food Safety* magazine,

> FSAI tested 14 food products with the scanner tool. One contained undeclared mustard at "significant levels." Mustard is considered an allergenic ingredient under EU and Irish food law. In another product, oregano actually contained DNA from two undeclared plant species. In yet another product, the plant species declared on the food label was not detected at all during the DNA scanning process.[40]

In addition to identifying unlabeled allergens, this DNA scanning tool could help officials detect whether certain foods are at a higher risk for containing foodborne pathogens. For example, in the past, DNA analysis has found that some beef products also contained meat from horses and that some products containing fish were mislabeled. If any products in mislabeled food were especially susceptible to foodborne pathogens, this could make the risk of getting sick from consuming them much higher.

Many consumers applaud the attempts of food suppliers and officials to improve the safety of the things people eat every day. In the meantime, people can take charge of their own health by taking simple precautions when cooking at home. Although foodborne pathogens are a serious matter, it is important for people to remember that the majority of the food they eat is safe for consumption and will remain that way as long as it is properly stored and prepared.

NOTES

Chapter One: Food Safety Throughout U.S. History

1. Quoted in Carol Ballentine, "Taste of Raspberries, Taste of Death: The 1937 Elixir Sulfanilamide Incident," *FDA Consumer*, June 1981. www.fda.gov/AboutFDA/History/ProductRegulation/ucm2007257.htm.

2. Quoted in Timothy Egan, *The Worst Hard Time: The Untold Story of Those Who Survived the Great American Dust Bowl*. Boston, MA: Houghton Mifflin, 2006, p. 256.

3. Michael Pollan, *The Omnivore's Dilemma: A Natural History of Four Meals*. New York, NY: Penguin Press, 2006, p. 49.

4. Mary Jane Brown, "Antibiotics in Your Food: Should You Be Concerned?," Healthline, June 17, 2017. www.healthline.com/nutrition/antibiotics-in-your-food.

5. "Remarks by the President in Radio Address to the Nation," The White House, Office of the Press Secretary, August 3, 1996. clintonwhitehouse3.archives.gov/CEQ/Record/080396speech.html.

6. Robert Tauxe, "Modern Meat," PBS *Frontline*, 2002. www.pbs.org/wgbh/pages/frontline/shows/meat/interviews/tauxe.html.

7. Eric Schlosser, *Fast Food Nation: The Dark Side of the All-American Meal*. New York, NY: Houghton Mifflin, 2001, p. 196.

8. Paul Roberts, *The End of Food*. New York, NY: Houghton Mifflin, 2008, p. 178.

9. Quoted in Roberts, *The End of Food*, p. 181.

10. Nicols Fox, *Spoiled: The Dangerous Truth About a Food Chain Gone Haywire*. New York, NY: Penguin Books, 1997, p. 8.

11. Quoted in Christopher D. Cook, *Diet for a Dead Planet: How the Food Industry Is Killing Us*. New York, NY: New Press, 2004, p. 49.

12. Quoted in Lyndsey Layton, "House Passes Legislation Overhauling Food-Safety Laws," *Washington Post*, December 21, 2010. www.washingtonpost.com/wp-dyn/content/article/2010/12/21/AR2010122104646.html.

Chapter Two: Food Safety Agencies in the United States

13. James T. O'Reilly, *A Consumer's Guide to Food Regulation & Safety*. New York, NY: Oceana/Oxford University Press, 2010, pp. 9–10.

14. Renée Johnson, *The Federal Food Safety System: A Primer*. Washington, DC: Congressional Research Service, December 16, 2016, p. 7. fas.org/sgp/crs/misc/RS22600.pdf.

15. O'Reilly, *A Consumer's Guide to Food Regulation & Safety*, p. 10.

Chapter Three: Foodborne Germs That Threaten America's Food Supply

16. Barbara Kowalcyk, "Kevin's Story," Center for Foodborne Illness, accessed on January 31, 2019. www.foodborneillness.org/kevin-s-story.html.

17. Roberts, *The End of Food*, p. 181.

18. Marion Nestle, *Safe Food: Bacteria, Biotechnology, and Bioterrorism*. Berkeley, CA: University of California Press, 2003, p. 35.

19. Roberts, *The End of Food*, p. 179.

Chapter Four: Reducing the Threat of Foodborne Pathogens

20. Diane Carmen, "Just Cook the Crud Out of It," *Denver Post*, July 26, 2002. gmwatch.org/en/news/archive/2002/2842-the-way-america-eats-just-cook-the-crud-out-of-it.

21. Terry D. Etherton, "Food Safety: Then and Now," *Animal Science Blogs*, August 2, 2011. sites.psu.edu/tetherton/2011/08/02/food-safety-then-and-now/

22. Quoted in "Do We Really Have a Food-Safety Crisis?," *Grist*, November 10, 2010. www.grist.org/article/food-2010-11-09-do-we-really-have-a-food-safety-crisis.

23. Quoted in "Water Troughs Are Key to E. Coli Contamination in Cattle," ScienceDaily, March 12, 2018. www.sciencedaily.com/releases/2018/03/180312150520.htm.

24. Warren Leon and Caroline Smith DeWaal, *Is Our Food Safe?: A Consumer's Guide to Protecting Your Health and the Environment*. New York, NY: Three Rivers Press, 2002, p. 27.

25. Quoted in "Definition of Food Irradiation," RxList, last updated December 11, 2018. www.rxlist.com/script/main/art.asp?articlekey=24431.

26. Quoted in Schlosser, *Fast Food Nation*, p. 218.

27. Quoted in Michael Janofsky, "U.S. Hopeful on Food Safety Efforts, but Critics Are Skeptical," *New York Times*, August 21, 1997. www.nytimes.com/1997/08/21/us/us-hopeful-on-food-safety-efforts-but-critics-are-skeptical.html?pagewanted=all&src=pm.

28. Roberts, *The End of Food*, p. 293.

29. Quoted in Timothy Donaghy, Francesca Grifo, Michael Halpern, and Heidi Moline, "Driving the Fox from the Henhouse: Improving Oversight of Food Safety at the FDA and USDA," Scientific Integrity Program of the Union of Concerned Scientists, September 2010, p. 24. www.ucsusa.org/sites/default/files/legacy/assets/documents/scientific_integrity/driving-fox-from-henhouse-food-safety-report.pdf.

30. Quoted in Christopher Doering, "Industry Has Sway Over Food Safety System: Study," Reuters, September 13, 2010. www.reuters.com/article/us-food-safety-study/industry-has-sway-over-food-safety-system-study-idUSTRE68C39320100913.

31. Ezra Klein, "Where's the Beef (Coming From)?," *Washington Post*, October 6, 2009. voices.washingtonpost.com/ezra-klein/2009/10/the_times_titled_this_article.html.

32. "The Essential Guide to FSMA," Safe Food Alliance, accessed on February 8, 2019. safefoodalliance.com/food-safety-resources/what-is-fsma/.

Chapter Five: The Food Technologies of the Future

33. "Food: Field to Fork," Pesticide Action Network, accessed on

February 8, 2019. www.panna.org/food-farming-derailed/food-field-fork.

34. Leon and DeWaal, *Is Our Food Safe?*, p. 102.

35. "EWG's 2019 Shopper's Guide to Pesticides in Produce," Environmental Working Group, March 20, 2019. www.ewg.org/foodnews/summary.php.

36. "Statement of Policy: Foods Derived from New Plant Varieties," Food and Drug Administration, *Federal Register*, vol. 57, no. 104. Washington, DC: Government Printing Office, May 29, 1992, pp. 22,984–22,985.

37. Dick Taverne, "The Real GM Food Scandal," *Prospect*, November 25, 2007. www.prospectmagazine.co.uk/2007/11/therealgmfoodscandal/.

38. Nestle, *Safe Food*, p. 173.

39. G. Owen Schaefer, "Lab-Grown Meat," *Scientific American*, September 14, 2018. www.scientificamerican.com/article/lab-grown-meat/.

40. "FSAI Now Using New DNA Technology to Identify Food Ingredients," *Food Safety*, February 25, 2019. www.foodsafetymagazine.com/news/fsai-now-using-dna-technology-to-identify-food-ingredients/.

North American Meat Institute
1150 Connecticut Avenue NW, 12th Floor
Washington, DC 20036
www.meatinstitute.org
twitter.com/MeatInstitute
www.youtube.com/user/meatnewsnetwork
> This organization is the country's oldest and largest meat and poultry trade association. It serves as the leading voice of American meat and poultry producers on all issues that affect its members, including safety and regulation matters.

Center for Food Safety
660 Pennsylvania Avenue SE, Suite 402
Washington, DC 20003
www.centerforfoodsafety.org
www.instagram.com/centerforfoodsafety
twitter.com/CFSTrueFood
www.youtube.com/user/centerforfoodsafety
> The Center for Food Safety describes itself as a nonprofit organization devoted to protecting human health and the environment by opposing genetically modified food and other food production technologies it considers harmful.

Food and Water Watch

1616 P Street NW, Suite 300

Washington, DC 20036

www.foodandwaterwatch.org

www.instagram.com/foodandwaterwatch

twitter.com/foodandwater

www.youtube.com/user/GoodFoodnH2O

    Food and Water Watch is a nonprofit consumer safety organization that monitors food and water quality throughout the United States and around the world. The group works to shape food and water regulations through a combination of education programs and lobbying efforts.

National 4-H Council

7100 Connecticut Avenue

Chevy Chase, MD 20815

4-h.org

www.instagram.com/national4h

twitter.com/4H

www.youtube.com/user/national4H

    4-H is the nation's largest development program for young people, empowering them with skills, education, and mentorship to help them become proactive members of their community.

Stop Foodborne Illness

4809 N. Ravenswood, Suite 214

Chicago, IL 60640

www.stopfoodborneillness.org

twitter.com/stopfoodillness

    This organization is dedicated to reducing foodborne illness and death across the United States. Its priorities range from stronger regulation of the food industry to helping people struggling with health problems from food poisoning.

Books

Bright, Michael. *From Field to Plate*. New York, NY: Crabtree Publishing, 2017.
> This book explores current farming and food processing methods to trace how food gets to restaurants and grocery stores.

Kivett, Joe, Mark Tamplin, and Gerald J. Kivett. *The Food Safety Book: What You Don't Know Could Kill You*. Orlando, FL: Constant Rose Publishing, 2016.
> This simple reference for basic issues on food safety provides consumers with information that could help them prevent foodborne illnesses in their homes.

Laine, Carolee. *Food Safety Basics*. Minneapolis, MN: Core Library, 2016.
> The author discusses the history and science of food safety. Pros and cons are presented to help readers make their own food decisions.

Pollan, Michael. *The Omnivore's Dilemma: Young Readers Edition*. St. Louis, MO: Turtleback Books, 2015.
> This is a kids' version of a best-selling book by one of America's most prominent food industry experts.

United States Food Safety and Inspection Service. *Food Safe Families Activity Book*. Washington, DC: United States Department of Agriculture, 2017.
> Through crossword puzzles, connect-the-dots, word scrambles, and other puzzles, this book teaches families about steps they can take in the kitchen to prevent food poisoning.

Websites

CDC: Food Safety

www.cdc.gov/foodsafety

> The CDC provides detailed information on outbreaks of foodborne illness as well as details on government food safety programs and regulations.

Fight BAC! Keep Food Safe from Bacteria

www.fightbac.org

> This website is maintained by the Partnership for Food Safety Education, which includes both consumer safety groups and food industry associations. It includes tips on handling food safely, educating kids about how foodborne illnesses are transmitted, and other consumer-targeted information.

FoodSafety.gov

www.foodsafety.gov

> This government website serves as a gateway to food safety information and alerts from all of the nation's leading food safety agencies.

Food Safety Project

www.extension.iastate.edu/foodsafety

> This comprehensive website maintained by Iowa State University is dedicated to food safety at all points of the food production and sale process. It includes information on safe food handling, trends in foodborne illness, and breaking food safety stories.

INDEX

PICTURE CREDITS

ABOUT THE AUTHOR

Juliana Burkhart is a native of Buffalo, NY, currently living in New York City. She teaches and performs acrobatics and hand balancing with a local circus troupe. She is a writer, artist, and dog-lover who enjoys spending time outdoors hiking and camping.